Teacher Certification Exam

English 7-12

Written By:

Mrs. Coleen St. Cyr., BS English
Joyce Kelly, PhD. English
Dorothea White, MS English

Edited By:
Marilyn C. Rinear, MS Education
BA English

To Order Additional Copies:
Xam, Inc.
99 Central St.
Worcester, MA 01605
Toll Free   1-800-301-4647
Phone: 1-508 363 0633
Email: winwin1111@aol.com
Web   www.xamonline.com
EFax   1-501-325-0185
Fax: 1-508-363-0634

You will find:
- Content Review in prose format
- Bibliography
- Sample Test

XAM, INC.
Building Better Teachers

"And, while there's no reason yet to panic, I think it's only prudent that we make preperations to panic."

Copyright © 2004 by XAM, Inc.

Note:
The opinions expressed in this publication should not be construed as representing the policy or position of the National Education Association, Educational Testing Service, or any State Department of Education. Materials published by XAM, Inc. are intended to be discussed documents for educators who are concerned with specialized interests of the profession.

All rights reserved. No part of this publication may be reproduced or transmitted in any form or by any means, electronic or mechanical, including photocopy, recording or any information storage or retrieval system, without permission in writing from the publisher, except where permitted by law or for the inclusion of brief quotations in the review.

Printed in the United States of America

CSET: English 7-12
ISBN: 1-58197-377-2

TEACHER CERTIFICATION EXAM

Competencies/Skills   **Page Numbers**

1.0 Knowledge of the English Language and effective teaching methods........2

    1.1 Demonstrate a comprehensive knowledge of the grammatical structure of the English language..2

    1.2 Identify various approaches to the teaching of grammar, language, and usage...19

    1.3 Demonstrate awareness of and differentiation between informative uses of language and manipulative uses of the English language..........25

    1.4 Demonstrate knowledge of historical, geographical, social, and personal factors that affect language usage..................................28

2.0 Demonstrate an understanding of writing and effective methods of teaching writing..32

    2.1 Integrate writing, reading, speaking, listening and viewing.....................32

    2.2 Recognize methods to create a classroom climate that encourages writing..34

    2.3 Demonstrate an understanding of the recursive aspects of the writing process...35

    2.4 Demonstrate an understanding of the methods for teaching students to write for a variety of aims and audiences...............................37

    2.5 Recognize methods for prewriting inquiries and organizing ideas (e.g., brainstorming, modeling, mapping, and webbing).................38

    2.6 Identify the techniques that cultivate among students a variety of proofreading, revising, and editing strategies.........................39

    2.7 Choose effective assessments of student writing....................................41

    2.8 Identify cooperative and peer activities that support the writing process...42

    2.9 Select effective responses to student writing..44

ENGLISH HIGH SCHOOL

Competencies/Skills **Page Numbers**

- 2.10 Understanding the function of grammar instruction in the context of writing and as one tool for teaching writing..................45

- 2.11 Demonstrate an understanding of the use of computer technology as it applies to the teaching of writing..................46

3.0 Knowledge of reading and effective teaching strategies..................49

- 3.1 Determine reading abilities and attitudes..................49

- 3.2 Demonstrate knowledge of teaching strategies for different types of reading material..................50

- 3.3 Select productive strategies for teaching vocabulary..................52

- 3.4 Demonstrate knowledge of reference sources for language and for literature..................54

4.0 Knowledge of literature and appropriate teaching strategies..................55

- 4.1 Demonstrate understanding of essential requisites of major literary genres..................55

- 4.2 Understand essential terminology for interpreting and explicating literature..................57

- 4.3 Comprehend major trends and the chronology of American literature, including major traditional and minority authors and their most acclaimed works..................63

- 4.4 Identification of fundamental characteristics of major multi-cultural writers including American Indian, Afro-American, Latino/a, and feminist..................69

- 4.5 Comprehend the major chronological movements of British literature through acclaimed works by renowned authors in each period..................73

- 4.6 Distinguish and identify major world writers and their works..................77

- 4.7 Demonstrate knowledge of adolescent literature and its relationship to adolescent development..................82

Competencies/Skills	Page Numbers

- 4.8 Identify elements of literature from which allusions are drawn...........97
- 4.9 Apply various critical responses to literature..100
- 4.10 Demonstrate knowledge of resources for literature criticism.................104
- 4.11 Identify and demonstrate a variety of methods for teaching literature..105

5.0 Demonstrate the ability to write competently on a topic..........................107

- 5.1 Write an essay reflecting literary skill...107

RESOURCES..118

Sample Teacher Certification Test..125

TEACHER CERTIFICATION EXAM

ENGLISH HIGH SCHOOL

THIS PAGE INTENTIONALLY LEFT BLANK.

COMPETENCY 1.0 KNOWLEDGE OF THE ENGLISH LANGUAGE AND EFFECTIVE TEACHING METHODS.

SKILL 1.1 Demonstrate a comprehensive knowledge of the grammatical structure of the English language.

It is assumed that any candidate for a certificate to teach language arts will have a thorough understanding of English grammar.

Test Format

Most teacher tests of professional knowledge of grammar will consist of either multiple-choice questions that require selecting an example of correct sentence structure, grammar, punctuation, capitalization, spelling, or usage from four or five options and/or an essay question that requires application of all grammatical skills. These questions may also require knowledge of traditional and non-traditional approaches to the study of grammar. Familiarity with terms such as prescriptive/ traditional, transformational/ generative, and structural grammars and recognition of their differences in the approaches to learning grammar are important concepts.

Areas of Review

To review rules of grammar in more depth, use any high school/college grammar textbook (Warriner's books or Strunk and White's *Elements of Style* are highly recommended).

SYNTAX

Sentence completeness

Avoid fragments and run-on sentences. Recognition of sentence elements necessary to make a complete thought, proper use of independent and dependent clauses (see *Use correct coordination and subordination*), and proper punctuation will correct such errors.

Sentence structure

Recognize simple, compound, complex, and compound-complex sentences. Use dependent (subordinate) and independent clauses correctly to create these sentence structures.

Simple	Joyce wrote a letter.
Compound	Joyce wrote a letter, and Dot drew a picture.
Complex	While Joyce wrote a letter, Dot drew a picture.
Compound/Complex	When Mother asked the girls to demonstrate their new-found skills, Joyce wrote a letter, and Dot drew a picture.

Note: Do **not** confuse compound sentence elements with compound sentences.

Simple sentence with compound subject
Joyce and Dot wrote letters.
The girl in row three and the boy next to her were passing notes across the aisle.

Simple sentence with compound predicate
Joyce wrote letters and drew pictures.
The captain of the high school debate team graduated with honors and studied broadcast journalism in college.

Simple sentence with compound object of preposition
Coleen graded the students' essays for style and mechanical accuracy.

Parallelism

Recognize parallel structures using phrases (prepositional, gerund, participial, and infinitive) and omissions from sentences that create the lack of parallelism.

Prepositional phrase/single modifier

Incorrect: Coleen ate the ice cream with enthusiasm and hurriedly.
Correct: Coleen ate the ice cream with enthusiasm and in a hurry.
Correct: Coleen ate the ice cream enthusiastically and hurriedly.

Participial phrase/infinitive phrase

Incorrect: After hiking for hours and to sweat profusely, Joe sat down to rest and drinking water.
Correct: After hiking for hours and sweating profusely, Joe sat down to rest and drink water.

Recognition of dangling modifiers

Dangling phrases are attached to sentence parts in such a way they create ambiguity and incorrectness of meaning.

Participial phrase

Incorrect: Hanging from her skirt, Dot tugged at a loose thread.
Correct: Dot tugged at a loose thread hanging from her skirt.

Incorrect: Relaxing in the bathtub, the telephone rang.
Correct: While I was relaxing in the bathtub, the telephone rang.

Infinitive phrase

Incorrect: To improve his behavior, the dean warned Fred.
Correct: The dean warned Fred to improve his behavior.

Prepositional phrase

Incorrect: On the floor, Father saw the dog eating table scraps.
Correct: Father saw the dog eating table scraps on the floor.

Recognition of syntactical redundancy or omission

These errors occur when superfluous words have been added to a sentence or key words have been omitted from a sentence.

Redundancy

Incorrect: Joyce made sure that when her plane arrived that she retrieved all of her luggage.
Correct: Joyce made sure that when her plane arrived she retrieved all of her luggage.

Incorrect: He was a mere skeleton of his former self.
Correct: He was a skeleton of his former self.

Omission

Incorrect: Dot opened her book, recited her textbook, and answered the teacher's subsequent question.
Correct: Dot opened her book, recited from the textbook, and answered the teacher's subsequent question.

Avoidance of double negatives

This error occurs from positioning two negatives that, in fact, cancel each other in meaning.

Incorrect: Harold couldn't care less whether he passes this class.
Correct: Harold could care less whether he passes this class.

Incorrect: Dot didn't have no double negatives in her paper.
Correct: Dot didn't have any double negatives in her paper.

TEACHER CERTIFICATION EXAM

Correct use of coordination and subordination

Connect independent clauses with the coordinating conjunctions - *and, but, or, for,* or *nor* - when their content is of equal importance. Use subordinating conjunctions - although, because, before, if, since, though, until, when, whenever, where - and relative pronouns - that, who, whom, which - to introduce clauses that express ideas that are subordinate to main ideas expressed in independent clauses. (See *Sentence Structure* above.)
Be sure to place the conjunctions so that they express the proper relationship between ideas (cause/effect, condition, time, space).

    Incorrect: Because mother scolded me, I was late.
    Correct: Mother scolded me because I was late.

    Incorrect: The sun rose after the fog lifted.
    Correct: The fog lifted after the sun rose.

Notice that placement of the conjunction can completely change the meaning of the sentence. Main emphasis is shifted by the change.

    Although Jenny was pleased, the teacher was disappointed.
    Although the teacher was disappointed, Jenny was pleased.

    The boys who wrote the essay won the contest.
    The boys who won the contest wrote the essay.

Note: While not syntactically incorrect, the second sentence makes it appear that the boys won the contest for something else before they wrote the essay.

ENGLISH HIGH SCHOOL

GRAMMAR

Subject-verb agreement

A verb agrees in number with its subject. Making them agree relies on the ability to properly identify the subject.

>One of the boys *was playing* too rough.
>No one in the class, not the teacher nor the students, was listening to the message from the intercom.
>The candidates, including a grandmother and a teenager, are debating some controversial issues.

If two singular subjects are connected by *and* the verb must be plural.

>A *man* and his *dog* were jogging on the beach.

If two singular subjects are connected by *or* or *nor*, a singular verb is required.

>Neither Dot nor Joyce has missed a day of school this year.
>Either Fran or Paul is missing.

If one singular subject and one plural subject are connected by *or* or *nor*, the verb agrees with the subject nearest to the verb.

>Neither the coach nor the players were able to sleep on the bus.

If the subject is a collective noun, its sense of number in the sentence determines the verb: singular if the noun represents a group or unit and plural if the noun represents individuals.

>The House of Representatives has adjourned for the holidays.

>The House of Representatives have failed to reach agreement on the subject of adjournment.

Use of verbs (tense)

Present tense is used to express that which is currently happening or is always true.

    Randy is playing the piano.

    Randy plays the piano like a pro.

Past tense is used to express action that occurred in a past time.

    Randy learned to play the piano when he was six years old.

Future tense is used to express action or a condition of future time.

    Randy will probably earn a music scholarship.

Present perfect tense is used to express action or a condition that started in the past and is continued to or completed in the present.

    Randy has practiced piano every day for the last ten years.

    Randy has never been bored with practice.

Past perfect tense expresses action or a condition that occurred as a precedent to some other action or condition.

    Randy had considered playing clarinet before he discovered the piano.

Future perfect tense expresses action that started in the past or the present and will conclude at some time in the future.

    By the time he goes to college, Randy will have been an accomplished pianist for more than half of his life.

Use of verbs (mood)

Indicative mood is used to make unconditional statements; subjunctive mood is used for conditional clauses or wish statements that pose conditions that are untrue. Verbs in subjunctive mood are plural with both singular and plural subjects.

> If I were a bird, I would fly.

> I wish I were as rich as Donald Trump.

Verb conjugation

The conjugation of verbs follow the patterns used in the discussion of tense above. However, the most frequent problems in verb use stem from the improper formation of past and past participial forms.

> Regular verb: believe, believed, (have) believed

> Irregular verbs: run, ran, run; sit, sat, sat; teach, taught, taught

Other problems stem from the use of verbs that are the same in some tense but have different forms and different meanings in other tenses.

> I lie on the ground. I lay on the ground yesterday. I have lain down.

> I lay the blanket on the bed. I laid the blanket there yesterday. I have laid the blanket every night.

> The sun rises. The sun rose. The sun has risen.

> He raises the flag. He raised the flag. He had raised the flag.

> I sit on the porch. I sat on the porch. I have sat in the porch swing.

> I set the plate on the table. I set the plate there yesterday. I had set the table before dinner.

Two other verb problems stem from misusing the preposition *of* for the verb auxiliary *have* and misusing the verb *ought* (now rare).

> Incorrect: I should of gone to bed.
> Correct: I should have gone to bed.

> Incorrect: He hadn't ought to get so angry.
> Correct: He ought not to get so angry.

Use of pronouns

A pronoun used as a subject of predicate nominative is in nominative case.

> She was the drum majorette. The lead trombonists were Joe and he.
> The band director accepted whoever could march in step.

A pronoun used as a direct object, indirect object of object of a preposition is in objective case.

> The teacher praised him. She gave him an A on the test. Her praise of him was appreciated. The students whom she did not praise will work harder next time.

Common pronoun errors occur from misuse of reflexive pronouns:

> Singular: *myself, yourself, herself, himself, itself*
> Plural: *ourselves, yourselves, themselves.*
>
> Incorrect: Jack cut hisself shaving.
> Correct: Jack cut himself shaving.
>
> Incorrect: They backed theirselves into a corner.
> Correct: They backed themselves into a corner.

Use of adjectives

An adjective should agree with its antecedent in number.

> Those apples are rotten. This one is ripe. These peaches are hard.

Comparative adjectives end in -er and superlatives in -est, with some exceptions like *worse* and *worst*. Some adjectives that cannot easily make comparative inflections are preceded by *more* and *most*.

> Mrs. Carmichael is the better of the two basketball coaches.
>
> That is the hastiest excuse you have ever contrived.
>
> Candy is the most beautiful baby.

Avoid double comparisons.

> Incorrect: This is the worstest headache I ever had.
> Correct: This is the worst headache I ever had.

When comparing one thing to others in a group, exclude the thing under comparison from the rest of the group.

> Incorrect: Joey is larger than any baby I have ever seen. (Since you have seen him, he cannot be larger than himself.)
> Correct: Joey is larger than <u>any other</u> baby I have ever seen.

Include all necessary word to make a comparison clear in meaning.

> I am as tall as my mother. I am as tall as she (is).
> My cats are better behaved than those of my neighbor.

MECHANICS

The candidate should be cognizant of proper rules and conventions of punctuation, capitalization, and spelling. Competency exams will generally test the ability to apply the more advanced skills; thus, a limited number of more frustrating rules are presented here. Rules should be applied according to the American style of English, i.e. spelling *theater* instead of *theatre* and placing terminal marks of punctuation almost exclusively within other marks of punctuation.

Punctuation

Using terminal punctuation in relation to quotation marks

In a quoted statement that is either declarative or imperative, place the period inside the closing quotation marks.

> "The airplane crashed on the runway during takeoff."

If the quotation is followed by other words in the sentence, place a comma inside the closing quotations marks and a period at the end of the sentence.

> "The airplane crashed on the runway during takeoff," said the announcer.

In most instances in which a quoted title or expression occurs at the end of a sentence, the period is placed before either the single or double quotation marks.

> "The middle school readers were unprepared to understand Bryant's poem 'Thanatopsis.'"

> Early book length adventure stories like *Don Quixote* and *The Three Musketeers* were known as "picaresque novels."

There is an instance in which the final quotation mark would precede the period - if the content of the sentence were about a speech or quote so that the understanding of the meaning would be confused by the placement of the period.

> The first thing out of his mouth was "Hi, I'm home."
> *but*
> The first line of his speech began "I arrived home to an empty house".

In sentences that are interrogatory or exclamatory, the question mark or exclamation point should be positioned outside the closing quotation marks if the quote itself is a statement or command or cited title.

> Who decided to lead us in the recitation of the "Pledge of Allegiance"?
>
> Why was Tillie shaking as she began her recitation, "Once upon a midnight dreary..."?
>
> I was embarrassed when Mrs. White said, "Your slip is showing"!

In sentences that are declarative but the quotation is a question or an exclamation, place the question mark or exclamation point inside the quotation marks.

> The hall monitor yelled, "Fire! Fire!"
>
> "Fire! Fire!" yelled the hall monitor.
>
> Cory shrieked, "Is there a mouse in the room?" (In this instance, the question supersedes the exclamation.)

Using periods with parentheses or brackets

Place the period inside the parentheses or brackets if they enclose a complete sentence, independent of the other sentences around it.

> Stephen Crane was a confirmed alcohol and drug addict. (He admitted as much to other journalists in Cuba.)

If the parenthetical expression is a statement inserted within another statement, the period in the enclosure is omitted.

> Mark Twain used the character Indian Joe (He also appeared in *The Adventures of Tom Sawyer*) as a foil for Jim in *The Adventures of Huckleberry Finn*.

When enclosed matter comes at the end of a sentence requiring quotation marks, place the period outside the parentheses or brackets.

> "The secretary of state consulted with the ambassador [Albright]."

Using commas

Separate two or more coordinate adjectives, modifying the same word and three or more nouns, phrases, or clauses in a list.

> Maggie's hair was dull, dirty, and lice-ridden.

> Dickens portrayed the Artful Dodger as skillful pickpocket, loyal follower of Fagin, and defendant of Oliver Twist.

> Ellen daydreamed about getting out of the rain, taking a shower, and eating a hot dinner.

> In Elizabethan England, Ben Johnson wrote comedy, Christopher Marlowe wrote tragedies, and William Shakespeare composed both.

Use commas to separate antithetical or complimentary expressions from the rest of the sentence.

> The veterinarian, not his assistant, would perform the delicate surgery.

> The more he knew about her, the less he wished he knew.

> Randy hopes to, and probably will, get an appointment to the Naval Academy.

> His thorough, though esoteric, scientific research could not easily be understood by high school students.

Using double quotation marks with other punctuation

Quotations - whether words, phrases, or clauses - should be punctuated according to the rules of the grammatical function they serve in the sentence.

> The works of Shakespeare, "the bard of Avon," have been contested as originating with other authors.

> "You'll get my money," the old man warned, "when 'Hell freezes over'."

> Sheila cited the passage that began "Four score and seven years ago...." (Note the ellipsis followed by an enclosed period.)

> "Old Ironsides" inspired the preservation of the U.S.S. Constitution.

Use quotation marks to enclose the titles of shorter works: songs, short poems, short stories, essays, and chapters of books. (See "Using Italics" for punctuating longer titles.)

"The Tell-Tale Heart"   "Casey at the Bat"   "America the Beautiful"

Using semicolons

Use semicolons to separate independent clauses when the second clause is introduced by a transitional adverb. (These clauses may also be written as separate sentences, preferably by placing the adverb within the second sentence.)

The Elizabethans modified the rhyme scheme of the sonnet; thus, it was called the English sonnet.
or
The Elizabethans modified the rhyme scheme of the sonnet. It thus was called the English sonnet.

Use semicolons to separate items in a series that are long and complex or have internal punctuation.

The Italian Renaissance produced masters in the fine arts: Dante Alighieri, author of the *Divine Comedy;* Leonardo da Vinci, painter of *The Last Supper;* and Donatello, sculptor of the *Quattro Coronati*, the four saints.

The leading scorers in the WNBA were Haizhaw Zheng, averaging 23.9 points per game; Lisa Leslie, 22; and Cynthia Cooper, 19.5.

Using colons

Place a colon at the beginning of a list of items. (Note its use in the sentence about Renaissance Italians on the previous page.)

The teacher directed us to compare Faulkner's three symbolic novels: *Absalom, Absalom; As I Lay Dying,* and *Light in August.*

Do **not** use a semicolon if the list is preceded by a verb.

Three of Faulkner's symbolic novels are *Absalom, Absalom; As I Lay Dying,* and *Light in August.*

Using dashes

Place dashes to denote sudden breaks in thought.

>Some periods in literature - the Romantic Age, for example - spanned different time periods in different countries.

Use dashes instead of commas if commas are already used elsewhere in the sentence for amplification or explanation.

>The Fireside Poets included three Brahmans - James Russell Lowell, Henry David Wadsworth, Oliver Wendell Holmes - and John Greenleaf Whittier.

Use italics to punctuate the titles of long works of literature, names of periodical publications, musical scores, works of art, and motion picture television, and radio programs. (When unable to write in italics, students should be instructed to underline in their own writing where italics would be appropriate.)

>*The Idylls of the King*   *Hiawatha*   *The Sound and the Fury*
>*Mary Poppins*   *Newsweek*   *The Nutcracker Suite*

Capitalization

Capitalize all proper names of persons (including specific organizations or agencies of government); places (countries, states, cities, parks, and specific geographical areas); and things (political parties, structures, historical and cultural terms, and calendar and time designations); and religious terms (any deity, revered person or group, sacred writings).

>Percy Bysshe Shelley, Argentina, Mount Rainier National Park, Grand Canyon, League of Nations, the Sears Towers, Birmingham, Lyric Theater, Americans, Midwesterners, Democrats, Renaissance, Boy Scouts of America, Easter, God, Bible, Dead Sea Scrolls, Koran

Capitalize proper adjectives and titles used with proper names.

California gold rush, President John Adams, French fries, Homeric epic, Romanesque architecture, Senator John Glenn

Note: Some words that represent titles and offices are not capitalized unless used with a proper name.

Capitalized	Not Capitalized
Congressman McKay	the congressman from Florida
Commander Alger	commander of the Pacific Fleet
Queen Elizabeth	the queen of England

Capitalize all main words in titles of works of literature, art, and music. (See "Using Italics" in the Punctuation section.)

Spelling

Concentration in this section will be on spelling plurals and possessives. The multiplicity and complexity of spelling rules based on phonics, letter doubling, and exceptions to rules - not mastered by adulthood - should be replaced by a good dictionary. As spelling mastery is also difficult for adolescents, our recommendation is the same. Learning the use of a dictionary and thesaurus will be a more rewarding use of time.

Most plurals of nouns that end in hard consonants or hard consonant sounds followed by a silent *e* are made by adding *s*. Some words ending in vowels only add *s*.

fingers, numerals, banks, bugs, riots, homes, gates, radios, bananas

Nouns that end in soft consonant sounds *s, j, x, z, ch,* and *sh*, add *es*. Some nouns ending in *o* add *es*.

dresses, waxes, churches, brushes, tomatoes

Nouns ending in *y* preceded by a vowel just add *s*.

boys, alleys

Nouns ending in *y* preceded by a consonant change the *y* to *I* and add *es*.

babies, corollaries, frugalities, poppies

Some nouns plurals are formed irregularly or remain the same.

>sheep, deer, children, leaves, oxen

Some nouns derived from foreign words, especially Latin, may make their plurals in two different ways - one of them Anglicized. Sometimes, the meanings are the same; other times, the two plurals are used in slightly different contexts. It is always wise to consult the dictionary.

>appendices, appendixes   criterion, criteria
>indexes, indices   crisis, crises

Make the plurals of closed (solid) compound words in the usual way except for words ending in *ful* which make their plurals on the root word.

>timelines, hairpins, cupsful

Make the plurals of open or hyphenated compounds by adding the change in inflection to the word that changes in number.

>fathers-in-law, courts-martial, masters of art, doctors of medicine

Make the plurals of letters, numbers, and abbreviations by adding *s*.

>fives and tens, IBMs, 1990s, *p*s and *q*s (Note that letters are italicized.)

Possessives

Make the possessives of singular nouns by adding an apostrophe followed by the letter *s* ('s).

>baby's bottle, father's job, elephant's eye, teacher's desk, sympathizer's protests, week's postponement

Make the possessive of singular nouns ending in *s* by adding either an apostrophe or a ('s) depending upon common usage or sound. When making the possessive causes difficulty, use a prepositional phrase instead. Even with the sibilant ending, with a few exceptions, it is advisable to use the ('s) construction.

>dress's color, species' characteristics or characteristics of the species, James' hat or James's hat, Delores's shirt

Make the possessive of plural nouns ending in *s* by adding the apostrophe after the *s*.

>horses' coats, jockeys' times, four days' time

Make possessives of plural nouns that do not end in *s* the same as singular nouns by adding '*s*.

> children's shoes, deer's antlers, cattle's horns

Make possessives of compound nouns by adding the inflection at the end of the word or phrase.

> the mayor of Los Angeles' campaign, the mailman's new truck, the mailmen's new trucks, my father-in-law's first wife, the keepsakes' values, several daughters-in-law's husbands

Note: Because a gerund functions as a noun, any noun preceding it and operating as a possessive adjective must reflect the necessary inflection. However, if the gerundive following the noun is a participle, no inflection is added.

> The general was perturbed by the private's sleeping on duty. (The word *sleeping* is a gerund, the object of the preposition *by*.

but

> The general was perturbed to see the private sleeping on duty. (The word *sleeping* is a participle modifying private.)

SKILL 1.2 Identify various approaches to the teaching of grammar, language, and usage.

Resources

Basic teaching texts used by teachers at large and found to be most helpful in teaching structure, grammar and composition:

Grades 7-12 - all students

Warriner's *Composition and Grammar: Fourth - First Course* and *Complete Course*, Orlando, FL: Harcourt, Brace, Jovanovich.

Intermediate to Advanced college-bound students and International-ESOL students

Oshima, Alice and Ann Hogue. *Writing Academic English* (Longman Series) *A Writing and Sentence Structure Handbook*. Reading, MA: Addison-Wesley Publications Co., 1991.

Grades 6-12

Hixon, Mamie W. *The Essentials of English Language*. Piscataway, New Jersey: Research and Education Association, 1995.

English Journal. Urbana, IL: National Council of Teachers of English.

Teachers will find numerous other published local resources in the school library or district resource centers.

Teaching Styles

Teaching styles are an extension of learning styles. Once teachers assess how students learn, they can vary their teaching styles to accommodate student needs. Research in the 1960s and 1970s solidified thinking about learning and teaching that had been evolving since the turn of the century. In the 1980s, several states adopted standards for student performance and began to hold teachers accountable for student progress. Formative and summative evaluation instruments were developed to enable administrators to evaluate teacher performance and to help teachers improve their teaching styles.

Six styles

1. **Task-oriented.** The teacher prescribes the resources and identifies specific performances, some of which may be individualized.

2. **Cooperation-centered.** The teacher and students plan the course of study and select resources together.

3. **Child-centered.** The student plans his own course of study based on his own interests.

4. **Subject-oriented.** Well-organized content dictates the course of study, with little regard to individual differences.

5. **Learning-centered.** This style combines both child-centered and subject-oriented approaches. The organized content and specific resources from which the student must select are prescribed.

6. **Emotionally exciting.** Not centered on any planning method, this style merely categorizes those teachers who instruct with more emotion than structure.

Concerns for the teacher

Within any of these styles, researchers identified specific element - instructional planning, personality traits, educational philosophy, attitudes toward students, teaching environments, methodology, and evaluation techniques - that could be assessed as having an impact on student learning.

As a result, in the last two decades, greater emphasis has been placed on identifying learning and teaching styles and attempting to match learner needs with the appropriate delivery methods. Teachers who have been trained and subscribe to task-oriented and subject-centered instruction are encouraged to abandon the textbook dependent or lecture approaches to learning in favor of smaller group discussion, independent study and research, and creative student projects. Teachers who have an abundance of enthusiasm, but little organization, have been encouraged to become more learning-oriented.

Early in each school year, the teacher needs to assess social, environmental, physical, and perceptual characteristics of each individual and class. This can be done informally through observation or formally with any number of learning style inventories. One inventory asks students to respond *true* or *false* to statements such as "Florescent light bothers my eyes" or "In a group, I always want to be the leader." Another inventory asks students to rank-order descriptive words that are indicators of positive or negative associations related to classroom environment, teacher qualities, student interests and abilities, and social skills.

The drawback of formal inventories is that adolescents aware of the inventory's purpose or youngsters who have been exposed to repeated assessments may intentionally or inadvertently miscue their responses. Many researchers and teachers prefer a hands-on approach to assessment. By trying various styles in the early weeks of a course of study, the teacher can observe the methods that work best. Using half a class as a control group or altering teaching styles with different classes during the day can result in providing improved instructional strategies and in making better recommendations for study techniques and resources for study.

LANGUAGE DEVELOPMENT

Learning approach

Early theories of language development were formulated from learning theory research. The assumption was that language development evolved from learning the rules of language structures and applying them through imitation and reinforcement. This approach also assumed that language, cognitive, and social developments were independent of each other. Thus, children were expected to learn language from patterning after adults who spoke and wrote Standard English. No allowance was made for communication through child jargon, idiomatic expressions, or grammatical and mechanical errors resulting from too strict adherence to the rules of inflection (*childs* instead of *children*) or conjugation (*runned* instead of *ran*). No association was made between physical and operational development and language mastery.

Linguistic approach

Studies spearheaded by Noam Chomsky in the 1950s formulated the theory that language ability is innate and develops through natural human maturation as environmental stimuli trigger acquisition of syntactical structures appropriate to each exposure level. The assumption of a hierarchy of syntax downplayed the significance of semantics. Because of the complexity of syntax and the relative speed with which children acquire language, linguists attributed language development to biological rather than cognitive or social influences.

Cognitive approach

Researchers in the 1970s proposed that language knowledge derives from both syntactic and semantic structures. Drawing on the studies of Piaget and other cognitive learning theorists (see Skill 4.7), supporters of the cognitive approach maintained that children acquire knowledge of linguistic structures after they have acquired the cognitive structures necessary to process language. For example, joining words for specific meaning necessitates sensory motor intelligence. The child must be able to coordinate movement and recognize objects before she can identify words to name the objects or word groups to describe the actions performed with those objects.

Adolescents must have developed the mental abilities for <u>organizing concepts as well as concrete operations</u>, <u>predicting outcomes</u>, and <u>theorizing</u> before they can assimilate and verbalize complex sentence structures, choose vocabulary for particular nuances of meaning, and examine semantic structures for tone and manipulative effect.

Sociocognitive approach

Other theorists in the 1970s proposed that language development results from sociolinguistic competence. Language, cognitive, and social knowledges are interactive elements of total human development. Emphasis on verbal communication as the medium for language expression resulted in the inclusion of speech activities in most language arts curricula.

Unlike previous approaches, the sociocognitive allowed that determining the appropriateness of language in given situations for specific listeners is as important as understanding semantic and syntactic structures. By engaging in conversation, children at all stages of development have opportunities to test their language skills, receive feedback, and make modifications. As a social activity, conversation is as structured by social order as grammar is structured by the rules of syntax. Conversation satisfies the learner's need to be heard and understood and to influence others. Thus, his choices of vocabulary, tone, and content are dictated by his ability to assess the language knowledge of his listeners. He is constantly applying his cognitive skills to using language in a social interaction. If the capacity to acquire language is inborn, without an environment in which to practice language, a child would not pass beyond grunts and gestures as did primitive man.

Of course, the varying degrees of environmental stimuli to which children are exposed at all age levels creates a slower or faster development of language. Some children are prepared to articulate concepts and recognize symbolism by the time they enter fifth grade because they have been exposed to challenging reading and conversations with well-spoken adults at home or in their social groups. Others are still trying to master the sight recognition skills and are not yet ready to combine words in complex patterns.

Concerns for the teacher

Because teachers must, by virtue of tradition and the dictates of the curriculum, teach grammar, usage, and writing as well as reading and later literature, the problem becomes when to teach what to whom. The profusion of approaches to teaching grammar alone are mind-boggling. In the universities, we learn about transformational grammar, stratificational grammar, sectoral grammar, etc. etc. But in practice, most teachers, supported by presentations in textbooks and by the methods they learned themselves, keep coming back to the same traditional prescriptive approach - read and imitate - or structural approach - learn the parts of speech, the parts of sentence, punctuation rules, sentence patterns. After enough of the terminology and rules are stored in the brain, then we learn to write and speak. For some educators, the best solution is the worst - don't teach grammar at all.

The same problems occur in teaching usage. How much can we demand students communicate in only Standard English? Different schools of thought suggest that a study of dialect and idiom and recognition of various jargons is a vital part of language development. Social pressures, especially on students in middle and junior high schools, to be accepted within their peer groups and to speak the non-standard language spoken outside the school make adolescents resistant to the corrective, remedial approach. In many communities where the immigrant populations are high, new words are entering English from other languages even as words and expressions that were common when we were children have become rare or archaic.

Regardless of differences of opinion concerning language development, it is safe to say that a language arts teacher will be most effective using the styles and approaches with which she is most comfortable. And, if she subscribes to a student-centered approach, she may find that the students have a lot to teach her and each other. Moffett and Wagner in the Fourth Edition of *Student-centered Language Arts K-12* stress the three I's: individualization, interaction, and integration. Essentially, they are supporting the sociocognitive approach to language development. By providing an opportunity for the student to select his own activities and resources, his instruction is individualized. By centering on and teaching each other, students are interactive. Finally, by allowing students to synthesize a variety of knowledge structures, they integrate them. The teacher's role becomes that of a facilitator.

Benefits of the sociocognitive approach

This approach has tended to guide the whole language movement, currently in fashion. Most basal readers utilize an integrated, cross-curricular approach to successful grammar, language, and usage. Reinforcement becomes an intradepartmental responsibility. Language incorporates diction and terminology across the curriculum. Standard usage is encouraged and supported by both the core classroom textbooks and current software for technology. Teachers need to acquaint themselves with the computer capabilities in their school district and at their individual school sites. Advances in new technologies require the teacher to familiarize herself with programs that would serve her students' needs. Students respond enthusiastically to technology. Several highly effective programs are available in various formats to assist students with initial instruction or remediation. Grammar texts, such as the Warriner's series, employ various methods to reach individual learning styles. The school library media center should become a focal point for individual exploration.

Professional growth

Attendance as a professional at language arts conferences should be an integral part of a teacher's life-long learning strategy. Shared enthusiasms, techniques, assessments, and materials result in an energized, focused instructor/facilitator. Technology conferences provide state-of-the-art, hands-on experiences for teachers to take back to students and the district administration who have the monies and need the direction on how best to spend them to serve the students. We highly encourage teachers to take the time to attend seminars, colloquies, in-services, and conventions. Encourage district in-service supervisors to include offerings that enable faculty members to receive updates from research professionals and to share innovations that are being developed within their own districts.

Also, plan on taking college courses to update teaching skills and methodology to help each student reach his potential. There are various writing and language arts programs specifically created by computer companies. Teachers need to review those available in their district and select those appropriate programs that assist with remediation or interest reluctant readers and writers.

SKILL 1.3 Demonstrate awareness of and differentiation between informative uses of language and manipulative uses of the English language.

By the time children begin to speak, they have begun to acquire the ability to use language to inform and manipulate. They have already used kinesthetic and verbal cues to attract attention when they seek some physical or emotional gratification. Children learn to apply names to objects and actions. They learn to use language to describe the persons and events in their lives and to express their feelings about the world around them.

Semantic connotations

To effectively teach language, it is necessary to understand that, as human beings acquire language, they realize that words have denotative and connotative meanings. Generally, denotative words point to things and connotative words deal with mental suggestions that the words convey. The word *skunk* has a denotative meaning if the speaker can point to the actual animal as he speaks the word and intends the word to identify the animal. *Skunk* has connotative meaning depending upon the tone of delivery, the socially acceptable attitudes about the animal, and the speaker's personal feelings about the animal.

Informative connotations

Informative connotations are definitions agreed upon by the society in which the learner operates. A *skunk* is "a black and white mammal of the weasel family with a pair of perineal glands which secrete a pungent odor." The *Merriam Webster Collegiate Dictionary* adds "...and offensive" odor. Identification of the color, species, and glandular characteristics are informative. The interpretation of the odor as *offensive* is affective.

Affective connotations

Affective connotations are the personal feelings a word arouses. A child who has no personal experience with a skunk and its odor or has had a pet skunk will feel differently about the word *skunk* than a child who has smelled the spray or been conditioned vicariously to associate offensiveness with the animal denoted *skunk*. The very fact that our society views a skunk as an animal to be avoided will affect the child's interpretation of the word. In fact, it is not necessary for one to have actually seen a skunk (that is, have a denotative understanding) to use the word in either connotative expression. For example, one child might call another child a skunk, connoting an unpleasant reaction (affective use) or, seeing another small black and white animal, call it a skunk based on the definition (informative use).

Using connotations

In everyday language, we attach affective meanings to words unconsciously; we exercise more conscious control of informative connotations. In the process of language development, the leaner must come not only to grasp the definitions of words but also to become more conscious of the affective connotations and how his listeners process these connotations. Gaining this conscious control over language makes it possible to use language appropriately in various situations and to evaluate its uses in literature and other forms of communication.

The manipulation of language for a variety of purposes is the goal of language instruction. Advertisers and satirists are especially conscious of the effect word choice has on their audiences. By evoking the proper responses from readers/listeners, we can prompt them to take action.

Choice of the medium through which the message is delivered to the receiver is a significant factor in controlling language. Spoken language relies as much on the gestures, facial expression, and tone of voice of the speaker as on the words he speaks. Slapstick comics can evoke laughter without speaking a word. Young children use body language overtly and older children more subtly to convey messages. These refinings of body language are paralleled by an ability to recognize and apply the nuances of spoken language. To work strictly with the written work, the writer must use words to imply the body language.

FORMS OF COMMUNICATION

Furthermore, it becomes the responsibility of the learner to understand the various structures of written/spoken communication, in order to refine the communication process.

> **Basic expository writing** simply gives information not previously known about a topic or is used to explain or define one. Facts, examples, statistics, cause and effect, direct tone, objective rather than subjective delivery, and non-emotional information is presented in a formal manner.
>
> **Descriptive writing** centers on person, place, or object, using concrete and sensory words to create a mood or impression and arranging details in a chronological or spatial sequence.
>
> **Narrative writing** is developed using an incident or anecdote or related series of events. Chronology, the 5 W's, topic sentence, and conclusion are essential ingredients.
>
> **Persuasive writing** implies the writer's ability to select vocabulary and arrange facts and opinions in such a way as to direct the actions of the listener/reader. Persuasive writing may incorporate exposition and narration as they illustrate the main idea.

Journalistic writing is theoretically free of author bias. It is essential when relaying information about an event, person, or thing that it be factual and objective. Provide students with an opportunity to examine newspapers and create their own. Many newspapers have educational programs that are offered free to schools.

Oral use of communication forms

Different from the basic writing forms of discourse is the art of debating, discussion, and conversation. The ability to use language and logic to convince the audience to accept your reasoning and to side with you is an art. This form of writing/speaking is extremely confined/structured, logically sequenced, with supporting reasons and evidence. At its best, it is the highest form of propaganda. A position statement, evidence, reason, evaluation and refutation are integral parts of this writing schema.

Interviewing provides opportunities for students to apply expository and informative communication. It teaches them how to structure questions to evoke fact-filled responses. Compiling the information from an interview into a biographical essay or speech helps students to list, sort, and arrange details in an orderly fashion.

Speeches that encourage them to describe persons, places, or events in their own lives or oral interpretations of literature help them sense the creativity and effort used by professional writers.

Useful resources

> Price, Brent - *Basic Composition Activities Kit* - provides practical suggestions and student guide sheets for use in the development of student writing.

> Simmons, John S., R.E. Shafer, and Gail B. West. (1976). *Decisions About The Teaching of English* - "Advertising, or Buy It, You'll Like It." Allyn & Bacon.

Additional resources may be found in the library, social studies, economic, debate and journalism textbooks and locally published newspapers.

SKILL 1.4 Demonstrate knowledge of historical, geographical, social, and personal factors that affect language usage.

Language, though an innate human ability, must be learned. Thus, the acquisition and use of language is subject to many influences on the learner. Linguists agree that language is first a vocal system of word symbols that enable a human to communicate his feelings, thoughts, and desires to other human beings. Language was instrumental in the development of all cultures and is influenced by the changes in these societies.

Historical influences

English is an Indo-European language that evolved through several periods. The origin of English dates to the settlement of the British Isles in the fifth and sixth centuries by Germanic tribes called the Angles, Saxons, and Jutes. The original Britons spoke a Celtic tongue while the Angles spoke a Germanic dialect. Modern English derives from the speech of the Anglo-Saxons who imposed not only their language but also their social customs and laws on their new land. From the fifth to the tenth century, Britain's language was the tongue we now refer to as Old English. During the next four centuries, the many French attempts at English conquest introduced many French words to English. However, the grammar and syntax of the language remained Germanic.

Middle English, most evident in the writings of Geoffrey Chaucer, dates loosely from 1066 to 1509. William Caxton brought the printing press to England in 1474 and increased literacy. Old English words required numerous inflections to indicate noun cases and plurals as well as verb conjugations. Middle English continued the use of many inflections and pronunciations that treated these inflections as separately pronounced syllables. English in 1300 would have been written "Olde Anglishe" with the *e*'s at the ends of the words pronounced as our short *a* vowel. Even adjectives had plural inflections: "long dai" became "longe daies" pronounced "long-a day-as." Spelling was phonetic, thus every vowel had multiple pronunciations, a fact that continues to affect the language.

Modern English dates from the introduction of The Great Vowels Shift because it created guidelines for spelling and pronunciation. Before the printing press, books were copied laboriously by hand; the language was subject to the individual interpretation of the scribes. Printers and subsequently lexicographers like Samuel Johnson and America's Noah Webster influenced the guidelines. As reading matter was mass produced, the reading public was forced to adopt the speech and writing habits developed by those who wrote and printed books.

Despite many students' insistence to the contrary, Shakespeare's writings are in Modern English. It is important to stress to students that language, like customs, morals, and other social factors, is constantly subject to change. Immigration, inventions, and cataclysmic events change language as much as any other facet of life affected by these changes. The domination of one race or nation over others can change a language significantly. Beginning with the colonization of the New World, English and Spanish became dominant languages in the Western hemisphere. American English today is somewhat different in pronunciation and sometimes vocabulary from British English. The British call a truck a "lorry;" baby carriages a "pram," short for "perambulator;" and an elevator a "lift." There are very few syntactical differences, and even the tonal qualities that were once so clearly different are converging.

Though Modern English is less complex than Middle English, having lost many unnecessary inflections, it is still considered difficult to learn because of its many exceptions to the rules. It has, however, become the world's dominant language by reason of the great political, military, and social power of England from the fifteenth to the nineteenth century and of America in the twentieth century.

Modern inventions - the telephone, phonograph, radio, television, and motion pictures - have especially affected English pronunciation. Regional dialects, once a hindrance to clear understanding, have fewer distinct characteristics. The speakers from different parts of the United States of America can be identified by their accents, but more and more as educators and media personalities stress uniform pronunciations and proper grammar, the differences are diminishing.

The English language has a more extensive vocabulary than any other language. Ours is a language of synonyms, words borrowed from other languages, and coined words - many of them introduced by the rapid expansion of technology.

It is important for students to understand that language is in constant flux. Emphasis should be placed on learning and using language for specific purposes and audiences. Negative criticism of a student's errors in word choice or sentence structures will inhibit creativity. Positive criticism that suggests ways to enhance communication skills will encourage exploration.

Geographical influences

Dialect differences are basically in pronunciation. Bostoners say "potty" for "party" and Southerners blend words like "you all" into "y'all." Besides the dialect differences already mentioned, the biggest geographical factors in American English stem from minor word choice variances. Depending on the region where you live, when you order a carbonated, syrupy beverage most generically called a soft drink, you might ask for a "soda" in the South, or a "pop" in the Midwest. If you order a soda in New York, then you will get a scoop of ice cream in your soft drink, while in other areas you would have to ask for a "float."

Social influences

Social influences are mostly those imposed by family, peer groups, and mass media. The economic and educational levels of families determine the properness of language use. Exposure to adults who encourage and assist children to speak well enhances readiness for other areas of learning and contributes to a child's ability to communicate his needs. Historically, children learned language, speech patterns, and grammar from members of the extended family just as he learned the rules of conduct within his family unit and community. In modern times, the mother in a nuclear family became the dominant force in influencing the child's development. With increasing social changes, many children are not receiving the proper guidance in all areas of development, especially language.

Those who are fortunate to be in educational day care programs like Head Start or in certified preschools develop better language skills than those whose care is entrusted to untrained care providers. Once a child enters elementary school, he is also greatly influenced by peer language. This peer influence becomes significant in adolescence as the use of teen jargon gives teenagers a sense of identity within his chosen group(s) and independence from the influence of adults. In some lower socio-economic groups, children use Standard English in school and street language outside the school. Some children of immigrant families become bilingual by necessity if no English is spoken in the home.

Research has shown a strong correlation between socio-economic characteristics and all areas of intellectual development. Traditional paper measurement instruments rely on verbal ability to establish intelligence. Research findings and test scores reflect that children, reared in nuclear families who provide cultural experiences and individual attention, become more language proficient than those who are denied that security and stimulation.

Personal influences

The rate of physical development and identifiable language disabilities also influence language development. Nutritional deficiencies, poor eyesight, and conditions such as stuttering or dyslexia can inhibit a child's ability to master language. Unless diagnosed early they can hamper communication into adulthood. These conditions also stymie the development of self-confidence and, therefore, the willingness to learn or to overcome the handicap. Children should receive proper diagnosis and positive corrective instruction.

In adolescence, the child's choice of role models and his decision about his future determines the growth of identity. Rapid physical and emotional changes and the stress of coping with the pressure of sexual awareness make concentration on any educational pursuits difficult. The easier the transition from childhood to adulthood, the better the competence will be in all learning areas.

Middle school and junior high school teachers are confronted by a student body ranging from fifth graders who are still childish to eighth or ninth graders who, if not in fact at least in their minds, are young adults. Teachers must approach language instruction as a social development tool with more emphasis on vocabulary acquisition, reading improvement, and speaking/writing skills. High school teachers can deal with the more formalized instruction of grammar, usage, and literature for older adolescents whose social development allows them to pay more attention to studies that will improve their chances for a better adult life.

As a tool, language must have relevance to the student's real environment. Many high schools have developed practical English classes for business/ vocational students whose specific needs are determined by their desire to enter the workforce upon graduation. More emphasis is placed upon accuracy of mechanics and understanding verbal and written directions because these are skills desired by employers. Writing résumés, completing forms, reading policy and operations manuals, and generating reports are some of the desired skills. Emphasis is placed on higher level thinking skills, including inferential thinking and literary interpretation, in literature classes for college-bound students.

COMPETENCY 2.0 DEMONSTRATE AN UNDERSTANDING OF WRITING AND EFFECTIVE METHODS OF TEACHING WRITING.

SKILL 2.1 Integrate writing, reading, speaking, listening and viewing.

The last twenty years have seen great change in instruction in the English classroom. Gone are the days when literature is taught on Monday, Wednesday is grammar day and Friday you assign writing. Integrating reading, writing, speaking, listening and viewing allows students to make connections between each aspect of language development.

Suggestions for Integrating Language Arts

- Use prereading activities such as discussion, writing, research, and journals. Use writing to tap into prior knowledge before students read; engage students in class discussions about themes, issues, and ideas explored in journals, predicting the outcome and exploring related information.

- Use prewriting activities such as reading model essays, researching, interviewing others, combining sentences and other prewriting activities. Remember that developing language proficiency is a recursive process and involves practice in reading, writing, thinking, speaking, listening and viewing.

- Create writing activities that are relevant to students by having them write and share with real audiences.

- Connect correctness - including developing skills of conventional usage, spelling, grammar, and punctuation - to the revision and editing stage of writing. Review of mechanics and punctuation can be done with mini-lessons that use sentences from student papers, sentence combining strategies, and modeling passages of skilled writers.

- Connect reading, writing, listening, speaking, and viewing by using literature read as a springboard for a variety of activities.

An example of an integrated creative writing lesson plan might begin with a discussion about lessons nature can teach us.

- Begin by exploring in a journal a lesson the students have learned from nature. (Writing/pre-reading/prior knowledge)

- Create a brainstorming chart/ cluster on the board from students' responses.

- Students would begin reading selections from NATURE by Ralph Emerson. (Reading)

- Discuss in class the connections. (Speaking/listening)

- Read aloud models of reflective essays on nature's lessons. Next students would go outside and, using a series of guided questions, observe an object in nature. (Writing/viewing)

- Use observations to allow students to write their own reflective essay on an object in nature. (writing) Use of peer response and editing would encourage students to share and improve their writing. (Writing/reading/speaking/listening)

- Read final pieces aloud to the class or publish them on a bulletin board.

SKILL 2.2 Recognize methods to create a classroom climate that encourages writing.

Viewing writing as a process allows teachers and students to see the writing classroom as a cooperative workshop where students and teachers encourage and support each other in each writing endeavor. Listed below are some techniques that help teachers to facilitate and create a supportive classroom environment.

1. Create peer response/support groups that are working on similar writing assignments. The members help each other in all stages of the writing process-from prewriting, writing, revising, editing, and publishing.

2. Provide several prompts to give students the freedom to write on a topic of their own. Writing should be generated out of personal experience and students should be introduced to in-class journals. One effective way to get into writing is to let them write often and freely about their own lives, without having to worry about grades or evaluation.

3. Respond in the form of a question whenever possible. Teacher/facilitator should respond noncritically and use positive, supportive language.

4. Respond to formal writing acknowledging the student's strengths and focusing on the composition skills demonstrated by the writing. A response should encourage the student by offering praise for what the student has done well. Give the student a focus for revision and demonstrate that the process of revision has applications in many other writing situations.

5. Provide students with readers' checklists so that students can write observational critiques of others' drafts, and then they can revise their own papers at home using the checklists as a guide.

6. Pair students so that they can give and receive responses. Pairing students keeps them aware of the role of an audience in the composing process and in evaluating stylistic effects.

7. Focus critical comments on aspects of the writing that can be observed in the writing. Comments like "I noticed you use the word 'is' frequently" will be more helpful than "Your introduction is dull" and will not demoralize the writer.

8. Provide the group with a series of questions to guide them through the group writing sessions.

SKILL 2.3 Demonstrate an understanding of the recursive aspects of the writing process.

STAGES OF WRITING

Writing is a recursive process. As students engage in the various stages of writing, they develop and improve not only their writing skills, but their thinking skills as well. The stages of the writing process are as follows:

PREWRITING

Students gather ideas before writing. Prewriting may include clustering, listing, brainstorming, mapping, free writing, and charting. Providing many ways for a student to develop ideas on a topic will increase his/her chances for success.

WRITING

Students compose the first draft.

REVISING

Students examine their work and make changes in sentences, wording, details and ideas. Revise comes from the Latin word *revidere*, meaning, "to see again."

EDITING

Students proofread the draft for punctuation and mechanical errors.

PUBLISHING

Students may have their work displayed on a bulletin board, read aloud in class, or printed in a literary magazine or school anthology.

It is important to realize that these steps are recursive; as a student engages in each aspect of the writing process, he or she may begin with prewriting, write, revise, write, revise, edit, and publish. They do not engage in this process in a lockstep manner; it is more circular.

TEACHING THE COMPOSING PROCESS

Prewriting Activities

1. Class discussion of the topic.
2. Map out ideas, questions, graphic organizers on the chalkboard.
3. Break into small groups to discuss different ways of approaching the topic and develop an organizational plan and create a thesis statement.
4. Research the topic if necessary.

Drafting/Revising

1. Students write first draft in class or at home.
2. Students engage in peer response and class discussion.
3. Using checklists or a rubric, students critique each other's writing and make suggestions for revising the writing.
4. Students revise the writing.

Editing and Proofreading

1. Students, working in pairs, analyze sentences for variety.
2. Students work in groups to read papers for punctuation and mechanics.
3. Students perform final edit.

SKILL 2.4 **Demonstrate an understanding of the methods for teaching students to write for a variety of aims and audiences.**

In the past teachers have assigned reports, paragraphs and essays that focused on the teacher as the audience with the purpose of explaining information. However, for students to be meaningfully engaged in their writing, they must write for a variety of reasons. Writing for different audiences and aims allows students to be more involved in their writing. If they write for the same audience and purpose, they will continue to see writing as just another assignment. Listed below are suggestions that give students an opportunity to write in more creative and critical ways.

* Write letters to the editor, to a college, to a friend, to another student that would be sent to the intended audience.

* Write stories that would be read aloud to a group (the class, another group of students, to a group of elementary school students) or published in a literary magazine or class anthology.

* Write plays that would be performed.

* Have students discuss the parallels between the different speech styles we use and writing styles for different readers or audiences.

* Allow students to write a particular piece for different audiences.

* Make sure students consider the following when analyzing the needs of their audience.

    1. Why is the audience reading my writing? Do they expect to be informed, amused or persuaded?
    2. What does my audience already know about my topic?
    3. What does the audience want or need to know? What will interest them?
    4. What type of language suits my readers?

* As part of the prewriting have students identify the audience.

    * Expose students to writing that is on the same topic but with a different audience and have them identify the variations in sentence structure and style.

* Remind your students that it is not necessary to identify all the specifics of the audience in the initial stage of the writing process but that at some point they must make some determinations about audience.

SKILL 2.5 Recognize methods for prewriting inquiries and organizing ideas (e.g., brainstorming, modeling, mapping and webbing).

Remind students that as they prewrite they need to consider their audience. Prewriting strategies assist students in a variety of ways. Listed below are the most common prewriting strategies students can use to explore, plan and write on a topic. It is important to remember when teaching these strategies that not all prewriting must eventually produce a finished piece of writing. In fact, in the initial lesson of teaching prewriting strategies, it might be more effective to have students practice prewriting strategies without the pressure of having to write a finished product.

* Keep an idea book so that they can jot down ideas that come to mind.

* Write in a daily journal.

* Write down whatever comes to mind; this is called free writing. Students do not stop to make corrections or interrupt the flow of ideas. A variation of this technique is focused free writing - writing on a specific topic - to prepare for an essay.

* Make a list of all ideas connected with their topic; this is called brainstorming. Make sure students know that this technique works best when they let their mind work freely. After completing the list, students should analyze the list to see if a pattern or way to group the ideas.

* Ask the questions Who? What? When? Where? When? and How? Help the writer approach a topic from several perspectives.

* Create a visual map on paper to gather ideas. Cluster circles and lines to show connections between ideas. Students should try to identify the relationship that exists between their ideas. If they cannot see the relationships, have them pair up, exchange papers and have their partners look for some related ideas.

* Observe details of sight, hearing, taste, touch, and taste.

* Visualize by making mental images of something and write down the details in a list

After they have practiced with each of these prewriting strategies, ask them to pick out the ones they prefer and ask them to discuss how they might use the techniques to help them with future writing assignments. It is important to remember that they can use more than one prewriting strategy at a time. Also they may find that different writing situations may suggest certain techniques.

SKILL 2.6 Identify techniques that cultivate among students a variety of proofreading, revising, and editing strategies.

Students need to be trained to become effective at proofreading, revising and editing strategies. Begin by training them using both desk-side and scheduled conferences. Listed below are some strategies to use to guide students through the final stages of the writing process.

* Provide some guide sheets or forms for students to use during peer responses.

* Allow students to work in pairs and limit the agenda.

* Model the use of the guide sheet or form for the entire class.

* Give students a time limit.

    - Have the students read their partners' papers and ask at least three who, what, when, why, how questions. The students answer the questions and use them as a place to begin discussing the piece.

Provide students with a series of questions that will assist them in revising their writing.

1. Do the details give a clear picture? Add details that appeal to more than just the sense of sight.

2. How effectively are the details organized? Reorder the details if it is needed.

3. Are the thoughts and feelings of the writer included? Add personal thoughts and feelings about the subject.

As you discuss revision, you begin with discussing the definition of revise. Also, state that all writing must be revised to improve it. After students have revised their writing, it is time for the final editing and proofreading. There are a few key points to remember when helping students learn to edit and proofread their work.

* It is crucial that students are not taught grammar in isolation, but in context of the writing process.

* At this point in the writing process a mini-lesson that focuses on some of the problems your students are having would be appropriate.

* Ask students to read their writing and check for specific errors like using a subordinate clause as a sentence.

* Provide students with a proofreading checklist to guide them as they edit their work.

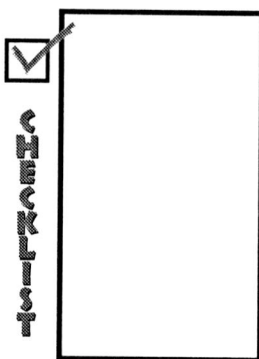

SKILL 2.7 Choose effective assessments of student writing.

When assessing and responding to student writing, there are several guidelines to remember.

Responding to non-graded writing (formative).

1. Avoid using a red pen. Whenever possible use a #2 pencil.
2. Explain the criteria that will be used for assessment in advance.
3. Read the writing once while asking the question is the student's response appropriate for the assignment?
4. Reread and make note at the end whether the student met the objective of the writing task.
5. Responses should be noncritical and use supportive and encouraging language.
6. Resist writing on or over the student's writing.
7. Highlight the ideas you wish to emphasize, question or verify.
8. Suggest and encourage your students to take risks.

Responding and evaluating graded writing (summative).

1. Ask students to submit prewriting and rough draft materials including all revisions with their final draft.
2. For the first reading, use a holistic method examining the work as a whole.
3. When reading the draft for the second time, assess it using the standards previously established.
4. Responses to the writing should be written in the margin and should use supportive language.
5. Make sure you address the process as well as the product. It is important that students value the learning process as well as the final product.
6. After scanning the piece a third time, write final comments at the end of the draft.

SKILL 2.8 Identify cooperative and peer activities that support the writing process.

The most recent research has reinforced what teachers have always known that cooperative learning is a powerful strategy in the classroom. Cooperative or collaborative learning is working together as we have always tried to do, but with a new understanding about how groups work together, borrowed from the areas of communication and psychology. Grouping can be a very effective way to work, but it can also be very ineffective. So, the question becomes how can I maximize the productivity of groups? While you are experimenting, keep the following ideas in mind.

1. Cooperative learning allows teachers to move away from the center of the room and rely less on lecturing.

2. Cooperative learning gives students the opportunity to verbalize their ideas.

3. Cooperative learning gives students more ownership of what they learn and therefore motivates them more.

Listed below are the group skills that you will want to emphasize when working it groups. Also, you will find three strategies that work. It is important to provide peer-evaluation guidelines.

Guidelines for the writer

- Make a list of questions or concerns for your peers.

- Maintain an open attitude. It is important to use the evaluator's comments rather than being defensive. Keep in mind that the readers are only trying to help you.

Guidelines for the peer-evaluator

- Begin by pointing out the strengths first. Then, identify the areas that need to be improved.

- Provide some encouragement as well as suggesting things the writer can do to improve the piece of writing.

- Focus on content and organization. Avoid commenting on errors of punctuation or mechanics. These problems can be fixed during the editing stage.

- Be sensitive to the writer's feelings as well as giving the peer-response your best effort.

TEACHER CERTIFICATION EXAM

When creating peer-response groups, keep in mind the following ideas.

1. Make sure each group is balanced with students of varying ability. Peer-response groups will not work effectively if all the strong writers are in one or two groups. Spread out the talents of the class evenly among the groups. It is usually better for the teacher to assign the groups because this method not only prevents hurt feelings, it also allows the teacher to balance the groups with varying academic abilities and skill levels to ensure maximum benefit for all students.

2. Allow the groups to work together for more than one session. It takes time to create a group that will work effectively together and for peers to become comfortable working together.

3. Don't expect groups to produce significant results initially. Remember evaluating and revising are the most demanding stages of writing.

SKILL 2.9 Select effective responses to student writing.

When responding to student writing, there are a variety of approaches you can use depending on the focus and purpose of the assignment. You may want to vary the approaches.

- Analytical Evaluation identifies the qualities of a successful piece of writing and attributes point values for each aspect. The student's grade is determined by the point total. Students often like this type of evaluation since it is concrete and highlights specific strengths and weaknesses. One drawback for this type of evaluation is that it places a greater emphasis on the part rather than the whole.

- Holistic Scoring assesses a piece of writing as a whole. Usually a paper is read quickly through once to get a general impression. The writing is graded according to the impression of the whole work rather than the sum of its parts. Often holistic scoring uses a rubric that establishes the overall criteria for a certain score to evaluate each paper.

- A Performance System identifies established criteria, and as long as the student meets the acceptable level of activity, the points are awarded. This particular approach is useful for activities like journal writing.

- Portfolio Grading allows the students to select the pieces of work to be graded. Often this technique is used with writing workshops. Students often like this method because they have control over the evaluation process. Also, since teachers do not have to grade everything, it lessens their workload.

When the time comes to assign grades, keep a few things in mind.

1. Each piece of writing should have clearly established criteria.

2. Involve students in the process of defining the criteria. Students are more apt to understand criteria they have helped develop.

3. Give students numerous experiences with formative evaluation (evaluation as the student is writing the piece). Give students points for the work they have done throughout the process.

4. During the summative evaluation phase (final evaluation), students play an active role. Provide them with a form to identify the best parts of the writing and the things they would work on given more time.

5. Focus on content, fluency and freshness of ideas with young writers. Correctness and punctuation will follow as they gain control of the language.

TEACHER CERTIFICATION EXAM

SKILL 2.10 Understanding the function of grammar instruction in the context of writing and as one tool for teaching writing.

Gone are the days when students engage in skill practice with grammar worksheets. Grammar needs to be taught in the context of the students' own work. Listed below is a series of classroom practices that encourage meaningful context-based grammar instruction, combined with occasional mini-lessons and other language strategies that can be used on a daily basis.

* Connect grammar with the student's own writing while emphasizing grammar as a significant aspect of effective writing.

* Emphasize the importance of editing and proofreading as an essential part of classroom activities.

* Provide students with an opportunity to practice editing and proofreading cooperatively.

* Give instruction in the form of 15-20 minute mini-lessons.

* Emphasize the sound of punctuation by connecting it to pitch, stress, and pause.

* Involve students in all facets of language learning including reading, writing, listening, speaking and thinking. Good use of language comes from exploring all forms of it on a regular basis.

There are a number of approaches that involve grammar instruction in the context of the writing.

1. Sentence Combining - try to use the student's own writing as much as possible. The theory behind combining ideas and the correct punctuation should be emphasized.

2. Sentence and paragraph modeling - provide students with the opportunity to practice imitating the style and syntax of professional writers.

3. Sentence transforming - give students an opportunity to change sentences from one form to another, i.e. from passive to active, inverting the sentence order, change forms of the words used.

4. Daily Language Practice - introduce or clarify common errors using daily language activities. Use actual student examples whenever possible. Correct and discuss the problems with grammar and usage.

SKILL 2.11 Demonstrate an understanding of the use of computer technology as it applies to the teaching of writing.

Current research indicates that the benefits of computer technology are that students spend more time on each piece of writing, that they feel free to experiment more, that they feel better about being able to manipulate their works on the monitor. However, the benefits and drawbacks of the computer as a part of the writing process need to be clarified.

Prewriting

Benefits

- According to research students spend more time on prewriting and planning since they can eliminate the distractions that handwriting and legibility create when they are developing their ideas.

- Computers provide students with programs that help young writers choose and explore a subject.

Drawbacks

- There is some research that suggests students actually spend less time prewriting.

- Writers who use computer assistance often focus on the sequence of ideas rather than the progression of ideas. The focus is placed on the order in which ideas are introduced rather than on the development of the ideas.

- It is difficult to manipulate some types of prewriting such as clustering on the computer.

- Young writers often read what they have written before ideas have had a chance to develop sufficiently. This can be prevented by turning down the resolution of the screen until the ideas have had a chance to develop.

The Bottom Line

- Since the use of the computer during prewriting might inhibit free flow of ideas, it is best to prewrite on paper. Changing from pen and paper to computer may open up new ideas for some writers.

Writing

Benefits

- The computer helps a writer stay with the writing longer and develop the ideas more completely.
- The computer allows writers to concentrate more on the ideas instead of the final product.

Drawbacks

- Some writers cannot refrain from making changes early in the drafting process and may disrupt the flow of their thoughts.

The Bottom Line

- Suggest that students draft work on the computer. If they cannot resist making changes, have them turn down the resolution on the computer screen.

Revising

Benefits

- The computer eliminates the need to rewrite or type the changes. This is especially helpful with longer essays and research papers.

- Revising is easier because a writer can move, delete, and add details with the stroke of a key.

Drawbacks

- The speed of the computer when making revisions can often discourage contemplation, exploring, and examination - the qualities of worthwhile writing.

The Bottom Line

- Advise your students to use the computer for revising and rewriting. Remind your students to allow for some time to ponder their writing during the revising process. Also, suggest that they have a printed copy on hand to make notes and to have another copy of the work after they have made revisions on the computer.

Editing and Proofreading

Benefits

- A computer promotes production of an error-free copy since making changes are so easy.

- There are a variety of programs available that aid students in preparing their work for final publication. Programs such as spell checkers and search and replace capabilities can be extremely helpful.

Drawbacks

- Again, the speed of the computer can encourage quickness, but not necessarily reflective writing.

- Spell check does no pick up misspellings such as using the word "too" when it should be "to" or "two."

The Bottom Line

- It is definitely a benefit to use the computer for the final stages of the writing process.

COMPETENCY 3.0 KNOWLEDGE OF READING AND EFFECTIVE TEACHING STRATEGIES.

SKILL 3.1 Determine reading abilities and attitudes.

George G. Spache; H. Alan Robinson; Edward B. Fry; Richard T. Vacca; Strang, McCullough, and Traxlor; and Delores Durkin are a select group of authors who provide the classroom teacher with concrete examples of "how to" provide insight into a student's reading style, skill development, interest, and other pertinent information regarding the individual student's needs. All this information will serve the classroom teacher in providing a challenging reading program for all.

These texts will assist the teacher to

- Provide appropriate material to meet the need of the student for instruction, enrichment, or remediation.

- Provide student-directed or teacher-directed activities in reading literature and content area curriculum texts.

- Provide resources and lessons that can provide a challenging opportunity for students to seek information from a wide variety of sources, such as television and computers.

- Provide suggestions and make recommendations that will foster a lifetime habit of seeking pleasure and knowledge from the printed word into the student.

- Provide the teacher an avenue of referral for students who are experiencing reading/learning disabilities and cannot have their needs met in the regular classroom setting. The inclusion of guidance counselors, speech pathologists, and school psychologists in a team approach are available in almost every school.

SKILL 3.2 Demonstrate knowledge of teaching strategies for different types of reading material.

In middle and secondary schools, the emphasis of reading instruction spans the range of comprehension skills - literal, inferential, and critical. Most instruction in grades five and six is based on the skills delineated in basal readers adopted for those grade levels. Reading instruction in grades seven through nine is usually part of the general language arts class instead of being a distinct subject in the curriculum, unless the instruction is remedial. Reading in tenth through twelfth grades is part of the literature curriculum - World, American, and British.

Reading emphasis in middle school

Reading for comprehension of factual material - content area textbooks, reference books, and newspapers - is closely related to study strategies in the middle/junior high. Organized study models, such as the SQ3R method, a technique that makes it possible and feasible to learn the content of even large amounts of text (Survey, Question, Read, Recite, and Review Studying), teach students to locate main ideas and supporting details, to recognize sequential order, to distinguish fact from opinion, and to determine cause/ effect relationships.

Strategies

1. Teacher-guided activities that require students to organize and to summarize information based on the author's explicit intent are pertinent strategies in middle grades. Evaluation techniques include oral and written responses to standardized or teacher-made worksheets.

2. Reading of fiction introduces and reinforces skills in inferring meaning from narration and description. Teaching-guided activities in the process of reading for meaning should be followed by cooperative planning of the skills to be studied and of the selection of reading resources. Many printed reading for comprehension instruments as well as individualized computer software programs exist to monitor the progress of acquiring comprehension skills.

3. Older middle school students should be given opportunities for more student-centered activities - individual and collaborative selection of reading choices based on student interest, small group discussions of selected works, and greater written expression. Evaluation techniques include teacher monitoring and observation of discussions and written work samples.

4. Certain students may begin some fundamental critical interpretation - recognizing fallacious reasoning in news media, examining the accuracy of news reports and advertising, explaining their reasons for preferring one author's writing to another's. Development of these skills may require a more learning-centered approach in which the teacher identifies a number of objectives and suggested resources from which the student may choose his course of study. Self-evaluation through a reading diary should be stressed. Teacher and peer evaluation of creative projects resulting from such study is encouraged.

5. Reading aloud before the entire class as a formal means of teacher evaluation should be phased out in favor of one-to-one tutoring or peer-assisted reading. Occasional sharing of favored selections by both teacher and willing students is a good oral interpretation basic.

Reading emphasis in high school

Students in high school literature classes should focus on interpretive and critical reading. Teachers should guide the study of the elements of inferential (interpretive) reading - drawing conclusions, predicting outcomes, and recognizing examples of specific genre characteristics, for example - and critical reading to judge the quality of the writer's work against recognized standards. At this level students should understand the skills of language and reading that they are expected to master and be able to evaluate their own progress.

Strategies

1. The teacher becomes more facilitator than instructor - helping the student to make a diagnosis of his own strengths and weaknesses, keeping a record of progress, and interacting with other students and the teacher in practicing skills.

2. Despite the requisites and prerequisites of most literature courses, students should be encouraged to pursue independent study and enrichment reading.

3. Ample opportunities should be provided for oral interpretation of literature, special projects in creative dramatics, writing for publication in school literary magazines or newspapers, and speech/debate activities. A student portfolio provides for teacher and peer evaluation.

SKILL 3.3 Select productive strategies for teaching vocabulary.

A planned, effective vocabulary program is not an "extra" but an across-the-curriculum necessity. The four-step process in such a program includes

1. Evaluate to determine what the students know.

2. Devise a plan to teach the students what they must learn as part of a continuum.

3. Determine if students have heard the words to be studied and in what context.

4. Teach vocabulary for MASTERY.

To reach mastery, clear-cut objectives and pacing are important since some students will need more practice than others. Building in time for practice, review, and testing is an integral component of a successful program.

Reteaching words missed on tests or misused in writing is essential until mastery is achieved.

The learning of vocabulary through visual, auditory, kinesthetic, and tactical experiences in a systematic order will enhance the learning process.

Methods of presentation, for a well-balanced program at all levels, include

- Recognizing and using words in context.

- Giving attention to varying definitions of the same word.

- Studying word families (synonyms, antonyms, and homonyms).

- Locating etymologies (word origins).

- Analyzing word parts (roots, prefixes, suffixes).

- Locating phonetic spellings and identifying correct pronunciation.

- Spelling words properly.

- Using words semantically.

Countless enrichment materials are available and include computer software, CD ROM, board games, flashcards, puzzles, etc. The more varied the experience, the easier and quicker students will commit the words to memory and mastery will be achieved.

The Shostak Vocabulary Series that spans middle school through grade 13, including SAT/ACT preparation is recommended by the authors for use in grades 9-12.

Within the literature series, vocabulary lists and practices are included. Classroom teachers should also review content area texts to add technical and specialized words to the weekly vocabulary study.

TEACHER CERTIFICATION EXAM

SKILL 3.4 Demonstrate knowledge of reference sources for language and for literature.

Titles listed in the resource list at the end of this guide are current references with which all language arts teachers should be familiar.

Though the list of literature text publishers is extensive, the following is a tried and true list that meets the needs of students in grades 6-12. Teachers should familiarize themselves with the texts adopted by their own districts and to select those resources that best reflect the district's scope and sequence.

- Heritage Edition Series - Harcourt Brace Jovanovich

- Norton Anthologies

- Bedford Introduction to Literature

- *Sound and Sense - Introduction to Poetry* | Laurence Perrine and R. Arp
- *Sound and Sense - Literature Structure*

- *Literary Cavalcade, Read,* and *Scholastic Magazine* - Scholastic supplemental reading

COMPETENCY 4.0 KNOWLEDGE OF LITERATURE AND APPROPRIATE TEACHING STRATEGIES.

SKILL 4.1 Demonstrate understanding of essential requisites of major literary genres.

The major literary genres include allegory, ballad, drama, epic, epistle, essay, fable, novel, poem, romance, and the short story.

Allegory: A story in verse or prose with characters representing virtues and vices. There are two meanings, symbolic and literal. John Bunyan's *The Pilgrim's Progress* is the most renowned of this genre.

Ballad: An *in media res* story told or sung, usually in verse and accompanied by music. Literary devices found in ballads include the refrain, or repeated section, and incremental repetition, or anaphora, for effect. Earliest forms were anonymous folk ballads. Later forms include Coleridge's Romantic masterpiece, "The Rime of the Ancient Mariner."

Drama: Plays – comedy, modern, or tragedy - typically in five acts. Traditionalists and neoclassicists adhere to Aristotle's unities of time, place and action. Plot development is advanced via dialogue. Literary devices include asides, soliloquies and the chorus representing public opinion. Greatest of all dramatists/playwrights is William Shakespeare. Other dramaturges include Ibsen, Williams, Miller, Shaw, Stoppard, Racine, Moliére, Sophocles, Aeschylus, Euripides, and Aristophanes.

Epic: Long poem usually of book length reflecting values inherent in the generative society. Epic devices include an invocation to a Muse for inspiration, purpose for writing, universal setting, protagonist and antagonist who possess supernatural strength and acumen, and interventions of a God or the gods. Understandably, there are very few epics: Homer's *Iliad* and *Odyssey*, Virgil's *Aeneid*, Milton's *Paradise Lost*, Spenser's *The Fairie Queene*, Barrett Browning's *Aurora Leigh*, and Pope's mock-epic, *The Rape of the Lock*.

Epistle: A letter that is not always originally intended for public distribution, but due to the fame of the sender and/or recipient, becomes public domain. Paul wrote epistles that were later placed in the <u>Bible</u>.

Essay: Typically a limited length prose work focusing on a topic and propounding a definite point of view and authoritative tone. Great essayists include Carlyle, Lamb, DeQuincy, Emerson and Montaigne, who is credited with defining this genre.

Fable: Terse tale offering up a moral or exemplum. Chaucer's "The Nun's Priest's Tale" is a fine example of a *bete fabliau* or beast fable in which animals speak and act characteristically human, illustrating human foibles.

Legend: A traditional narrative or collection of related narratives, popularly regarded as historically factual but actually a mixture of fact and fiction.

Myth: Stories that are more or less universally shared within a culture to explain its history and traditions.

Novel: The longest form of fictional prose containing a variety of characterizations, settings, local color and regionalism. Most have complex plots, expanded description, and attention to detail. Some of the great novelists include Austin, the Brontes, Twain, Tolstoy, Hugo, Hardy, Dickens, Hawthorne, Forster, and Flaubert.

Poem: The only requirement is rhythm. Sub-genres include fixed types of literature such as the sonnet, elegy, ode, pastoral, and villanelle. Unfixed types of literature include blank verse and dramatic monologue.

Romance: A highly imaginative tale set in a fantastical realm dealing with the conflicts between heroes, villains and/or monsters. "The Knight's Tale" from Chaucer's *Canterbury Tales*, *Sir Gawain and the Green Knight* and Keats' "The Eve of St. Agnes" are prime representatives.

Short Story: Typically a terse narrative, with less developmental background about characters. May include description, author's point of view, and tone. Poe emphasized that a successful short story should create one focused impact. Considered to be great short story writers are Hemingway, Faulkner, Twain, Joyce, Shirley Jackson, Flannery O'Connor, de Maupasssant, Saki, Edgar Allen Poe, and Pushkin.

SKILL 4.2 Understand essential terminology for interpreting and explicating literature.

Essential terminology and literary devices germane to literary analysis include alliteration, allusion, antithesis, aphorism, apostrophe, assonance, blank verse, caesura, conceit, connotation, consonance, couplet, denotation, diction, epiphany, exposition, figurative language, free verse, hyperbole, iambic pentameter, inversion, irony, kenning, metaphor, metaphysical poetry, metonymy, motif, onomatopoeia, octava rima, oxymoron, paradox, parallelism personification, quatrain, scansion, simile, soliloquy, Spenserian stanza, synecdoche, terza rima, tone, and wit.

The more basic terms and devices, such as alliteration, allusion, analogy, aside, assonance, atmosphere, climax, consonance, denouement, elegy, foil, foreshadowing, metaphor, simile, setting, symbol, and theme are defined and exemplified in the English 5-9 Study Guide.

Antithesis: Balanced writing about conflicting ideas, usually expressed in sentence form. Some examples are expanding from the center, shedding old habits, and searching never finding.

Aphorism: A focused, succinct expression about life from a sagacious viewpoint. Writings by Ben Franklin, Sir Francis Bacon, and Alexander Pope contain many aphorisms. "Whatever is begun in anger ends in shame" is an aphorism.

Apostrophe: Literary device of addressing an absent or dead person, an abstract idea, or an inanimate object. Sonneteers, such as Sir Thomas Wyatt, John Keats, and William Wordsworth, address the moon, stars, and the dead Milton. For example, in William Shakespeare's *Julius Caesar*, Mark Antony addresses the corpse of Caesar in the speech that begins: "O, pardon me, thou bleeding piece of earth, That I am meek and gentle with these butchers! Thou art the ruins of the noblest man That ever lived in the tide of times. Woe to the hand that shed this costly blood!"

Blank Verse: Poetry written in iambic pentameter but unrhymed. Works by Shakespeare and Milton are epitomes of blank verse. Milton's Paradise Lost states, "Illumine, what is low raise and support, That to the highth of this great argument I may assert Eternal Providence And justify the ways of God to men."

Caesura: A pause, usually signaled by punctuation, in a line of poetry. The earliest usage occurs in *Beowulf*, the first English epic dating from the Anglo-Saxon era. 'To err is human, // to forgive, divine' (Pope).

TEACHER CERTIFICATION EXAM

Conceit: A comparison, usually in verse, between seemingly disparate objects or concepts. John Donne's metaphysical poetry contains many clever conceits. For instance, Donne's "The Flea" (1633) compares a flea bite to the act of love; and in "A Valediction: Forbidding Mourning" (1633) separated lovers are likened to the legs of a compass, the leg drawing the circle eventually returning home to "the fixed foot."

Connotation: The ripple effect surrounding the implications and associations of a given word, distinct from the denotative, or literal meaning. For example, Good noght, sweet prince, and flights of angels sing thee to thy *rest* refers to a burial.

Consonance: The repeated usage of similar consonant sounds, most often used in poetry. "Sally sat sifting seashells by the seashore" is a familiar example.

Couplet: Two rhyming lines of poetry. Shakespeare's sonnets end in heroic couplets written in iambic pentameter. Pope is also a master of the couplet. His *Rape of the Lock* is written entirely in heroic couplets.

Denotation: What a word literally means, as opposed to its connotative meaning. For example, Good night, sweet prince, and flights of angels sing thee to thy *rest* refers to sleep.

Diction: The right word in the right spot for the right purpose. The hallmark of a great writer is precise, unusual, and memorable diction.

Epiphany: The moment when the proverbial light bulb goes off in one's head and comprehension sets in.

Exposition: Fill-in or background information about characters meant to clarify and add to the narrative; the initial plot element which precedes the buildup of conflict.

Figurative Language: Not meant in a literal sense, but to be interpreted through symbolism. Figurative language is made up of such literary devices as hyperbole, metonymy, synecdoche, and oxymoron. A synecdoche is a figure of speech in which the word for part of something is used to mean the whole; for example, "sail" for "boat," or vice versa.

Free Verse: Poetry that does not have any predictable meter or patterning. Margaret Atwood, e. e. cummings, and Ted Hughes write in this form.

Hyperbole: Exaggeration for a specific effect. For example, "I could eat a million of these."

Iambic Pentameter: The two elements in a set five-foot line of poetry. An iamb is two syllables, unaccented and accented, per foot or measure. Pentameter means five feet of these iambs per line or ten syllables.

Inversion: A typical sentence order to create a given effect or interest. Bacon and Milton's work use inversion successfully. Emily Dickinson was fond of arranging words outside of their familiar order. For example in "Chartless" she writes "Yet know I how the heather looks" and "Yet certain am I of the spot." Instead of saying "Yet I know" and "Yet I am certain" she reverses the usual order and shifts the emphasis to the more important words.

Irony: An unexpected disparity between what is written or stated and what is really meant or implied by the author. Verbal, situational, and dramatic are the three literary ironies. Verbal irony is when an author says one thing and means something else. Dramatic irony is when an audience perceives something that a character in the literature does not know. Irony of situation is a discrepancy between the expected result and actual results. Shakespeare's plays contain numerous and highly effective use of irony. O. Henry's short stories have ironic endings.

Kenning: Another way to describe a person, place, or thing so as to avoid prosaic repetition. The earliest examples can be found in Anglo-Saxon literature such as *Beowulf* and "The Seafarer." Instead of writing King Hrothgar, the anonymous monk wrote, great Ring-Giver, or Father of his people. A lake becomes the swans' way, and the ocean or sea becomes the great whale's way. In ancient Greek literature, this device was called an "epithet."

Metaphysical Poetry: Verse characterization by ingenious wit, unparalleled imagery, and clever conceits. The greatest metaphysical poet is John Donne. Henry Vaughn and other 17th century British poets contributed to this movement as in *Words*, "I saw eternity the other night, like a great being of pure and endless light."

Metonymy: Use of an object or idea closely identified with another object or idea to represent the second. "Hit the books" means "go study." Washington, D.C. means the U.S. government and the White House means the U.S. President.

Motif: A key, oft-repeated phrase, name, or idea in a literary work. Dorset/Wessex in Hardy's novels and the moors and the harsh weather in the Bronte sisters' novels are effective use of motifs. Shakespeare's *Romeo and Juliet* represents the ill-fated young lovers' motif.

Onomatopoeia: Word used to evoke the sound in its meaning. The early Batman series used *pow, zap, whop, zonk* and *eek* in an onomatopoetic way.

Octava rima: A specific eight-line stanza of poetry whose rhyme scheme is abababcc. Lord Byron's mock epic, *Don Juan*, is written in this poetic way.

Oxymoron: A contradictory form of speech, such as jumbo shrimp, unkindly kind, or Mellencamp's "It hurts so good."

Paradox: Seemingly untrue statement, which when examined more closely proves to be true. John Donne's sonnet "Death Be Not Proud" postulates that death shall die and humans will triumph over death, at first thought not true, but ultimately explained and proven in this sonnet.

Parallelism: A type of close repetition of clauses or phrases that emphasize key topics or ideas in writing. The psalms in the King James Version of the *Bible* contain many examples.

Personification: Giving human characteristics to inanimate objects or concepts. Great writers, with few exceptions, are masters of this literary device.

Quatrain: A poetic stanza composed of four lines. A Shakespearean or Elizabethan sonnet is made up of three quatrains and ends with a heroic couplet.

Scansion: The two-part analysis of a poetic line. Count the number of syllables per line and determine where the accents fall. Divide the line into metric feet. Name the meter by the type and number of feet. Much is written about scanning poetry. Try not to inundate your students with this jargon; rather allow them to feel the power of the poets' words, ideas, and images instead.

Soliloquy: A highlighted speech, in drama, usually delivered by a major character expounding on the author's philosophy or expressing, at times, universal truths. This is done with the character alone on the stage.

Spenserian Stanza: Invented by Sir Edmund Spenser for usage in *The Fairie Queene*, his epic poem honoring Queen Elizabeth I. Each stanza consists of nine lines, eight in iambic parameter. The ninth line, called an alexandrine, has two extra syllables or one additional foot.

Sprung Rhythm: Invented and used extensively by the poet, Gerard Manley Hopkins. It consists of variable meter, which combines stressed and unstressed syllables fashioned by the author. See "Pied Beauty" or "God's Grandeur."

Stream of Consciousness: A style of writing which reflects the mental processes of the characters expressing, at times, jumbled memories, feelings, and dreams. "Big time players" in this type of expression are James Joyce, Virginia Woolf, and William Faulkner.

Terza Rima: A series of poetic stanzas utilizing the recurrent rhyme scheme of aba, bcb, cdc, ded, and so forth. The second-generation Romantic poets - Keats, Byron, Shelley, and, to a lesser degree, Yeats - used this Italian verse form, especially in their odes. Dante used this stanza in *The Divine Comedy*.

Tone: The discernible attitude inherent in an author's work regarding the subject, readership, or characters. Swift's or Pope's tone is satirical. Boswell's tone toward Johnson is admiring.

Wit: Writing of genius, keenness, and sagacity expressed through clever use of language. Alexander Pope and the Augustans wrote about and were themselves said to possess wit.

In addition to these terms, there are four major time periods of writings. They are neoclassicism, romanticism, realism, and naturalism. Certain authors, among these Chaucer, Shakespeare, Whitman, Dickinson, and Donne, though writing during a particular literary period, are considered to have a style all their own.

Neoclassicism: Patterned after the greatest writings of classical Greece and Rome, this type of writing is characterized by balanced, graceful, well-crafted, refined, elevated style. Major proponents of this style are poet laureates, John Dryden and Alexander Pope. The eras in which they wrote are called the Ages of Dryden and Pope. The self is not exalted and focus is on the group, not the individual, in neoclassic writing.

Romanticism: Writings emphasizing the individual. Emotions and feelings are validated. Nature acts as an inspiration for creativity; it is a balm of the spirit. Romantics hearken back to medieval, chivalric themes and ambiance. They also emphasize supernatural, Gothic themes and settings, which are characterized by gloom and darkness. Imagination is stressed. New types of writings include detective and horror stories (Poe) and autobiographical introspection (Wordsworth and Thoreau). There are two generations in British Literature: First Generation includes William Wordsworth and Samuel Taylor Coleridge whose collaboration, *Lyrical Ballads*, defines romanticism and its exponents. Wordsworth maintained that the scenes and events of everyday life and the speech of ordinary people were the raw material of which poetry could and should be made. Romanticism spread to the United States, where Ralph Waldo Emerson and Henry David Thoreau adopted it in their transcendental romanticism, emphasizing reasoning. Further extensions of this style are found in Edgar Allan Poe's Gothic writings. Second Generation romantics include the ill-fated Englishmen Lord Byron, John Keats, and Percy Bysshe Shelley. Lord Byron and Percy Bysshe Shelley, who for some most typify the romantic poet (in their personal lives as well as in their work), wrote resoundingly in protest against social and political wrongs and in defense of the struggles for liberty in Italy and Greece. The Second Generation romantics stressed personal introspection and the love of beauty and nature as requisites of inspiration.

Realism: Unlike classical and neoclassical writing which, often deal with aristocracies and nobility or the gods, realistic writers deal with the common man and his socio/economic problems in a non-sentimental way. Muckraking, social injustice, domestic abuse, and inner city conflicts are examples of writings by writers of realism. Realistic writers include Stephen Crane, Ernest Hemingway, Thomas Hardy, George Bernard Shaw, and Henrik Ibsen.

Naturalism: This is realism pushed to the maximum, writing which exposes the underbelly of society, usually the lower class struggles. This is the world of penury, injustice, abuse, ghetto survival, hungry children, single parenting, and substance abuse. Émile Zola was inspired by his readings in history and medicine and attempted to apply methods of scientific observation to the depiction of pathological human character, notably in his series of novels devoted to several generations of one French family.

SKILL 4.3 **Comprehend major trends and the chronology of American literature, including major traditional and minority authors and their most acclaimed works.**

American Literature is defined by a number of clearly identifiable periods.

1. Native American works from various tribes

These were originally part of a vast oral tradition that spanned most of continental America from as far back as before the 15th century.

- Characteristics of native Indian literature include
  - reverence for and awe of nature.
  - the interconnectedness of the elements in the life cycle.

- Themes of Indian literature often reflect
  - the hardiness of the native body and soul.
  - remorse for the destruction of their way of life.
  - the genocide of many tribes by the encroaching settlement and Manifest Destiny policies of the U. S. government.

2. The Colonial Period in both New England and the South

Stylistically, early colonists' writings were neo-classical, emphasizing order, balance, clarity, and reason. Schooled in England, their writing and speaking was still decidedly British even as their thinking became entirely American.

Early American literature reveals the lives and experiences of the New England expatriates who left England to find religious freedom.

William Bradford's excerpts from *The Mayflower Compact* relate vividly the hardships of crossing the Atlantic in such a tiny vessel, the misery and suffering of the first winter, the approaches of the American Indians, the decimation of their ranks, and the establishment of the Bay Colony of Massachusetts.

Anne Bradstreet's poetry relates much concerning colonial New England life. From her journals, modern readers learn of the everyday life of the early settlers, the hardships of travel, and the responsibilities of different groups and individuals in the community,

Early American literature also reveals the commercial and political adventures of the Cavaliers who came to the New World with King George's blessing.

William Byrd's journal, *A History of the Dividing Line,* concerning his trek into the Dismal Swamp separating the Carolinian territories from Virginia and Maryland makes quite lively reading. A privileged insider to the English Royal Court, Byrd, like other Southern Cavaliers, was given grants to pursue business ventures.

The Revolutionary Period contains non-fiction genres: essay, pamphlet, speech, famous document, and epistle.

Major writers and works of the Revolutionary Period:

Thomas Paine's pamphlet, Common *Sense*, which, though written by a recently transplanted Englishman, spoke to the American patriots' common sense in dealing with the issues in the cause of freedom.

Other contributions are Benjamin Franklin's essays from *Poor Richard's Almanac* and satires such as "How to Reduce a Great Empire to a Small One" and "A Letter to Madame Gout."

There were great orations such as Patrick Henry's *Speech to the Virginia House of Burgesses* -- the "Give me liberty or give me death" speech - and George Washington's *Farewell to the Army of the Potomac*. Less memorable and thought rambling by modern readers are Washington's inaugural addresses.

The *Declaration of Independence*, the brainchild predominantly of Thomas Jefferson, with some prudent editing by Ben Franklin, is a prime example of neoclassical writing -- balanced, well crafted, and focused.

Epistles include the exquisitely written, moving correspondence between John Adams and Abigail Adams. The poignancy of their separation - she in Boston, he in Philadelphia - is palpable and real.

3. The Romantic Period

Early American folktales, and the emergence of a distinctly American writing, not just a stepchild to English forms, constitute the next period.

Washington Irving's characters, Icabod Crane and Rip Van Winkle, create a uniquely American folklore devoid of English influences. The characters are indelibly marked by their environment and the superstitions of the New Englander. The early American writings of James Fenimore Cooper and his Leatherstocking Tales with their stirring accounts of drums along the Mohawk and the French and Indian Wars, the futile British defense of Fort William Henry and the brutalities of this time frame allow readers a window into their uniquely American world. Natty Bumppo, Chingachgook, Uncas, and Magua are unforgettable characters that reflect the American spirit in thought and action.

The poetry of Fireside Poets - James Russell Lowell, Oliver Wendell Holmes, Henry Wadsworth Longfellow, and John Greenleaf Whittier - was recited by American families and read in the long New England winters. In "The Courtin'," Lowell used Yankee dialect to tell a narrative. Spellbinding epics by Longfellow such as *Hiawatha*, *The Courtship of Miles Standish*, and *Evangeline* told of adversity, sorrow, and ultimate happiness in an uniquely American warp. "Snowbound" by Whittier relates the story of a captive family isolated by a blizzard, stressing family closeness. Holmes' "The Chambered Nautilus" and his famous line, "Fired the shot heard round the world," put American poetry on a firm footing with other world writers.

Nathaniel Hawthorne and Herman Melville are the preeminent early American novelists, writing on subjects definitely regional, specific and American, yet sharing insights about human foibles, fears, loves, doubts, and triumphs. Hawthorne's writings range from children's stories, like the Cricket on the Hearth series, to adult fare of dark brooding short stories such as "Dr. Heidegger's Experiment," "The Devil and Tom Walker," and "Rapuccini's Daughter." His masterpiece, *The Scarlet Letter*, takes in the society of hypocritical Puritan New Englanders, who ostensibly left England to establish religious freedom, but who have been entrenched in judgmental finger wagging. They ostracize Hester and condemn her child, Pearl, as a child of Satan. Great love, sacrifice, loyalty, suffering, and related epiphanies add universality to this tale. *The House of the Seven Gables* also deals with kept secrets, loneliness, societal pariahs, and love ultimately triumphing over horrible wrong. Herman Melville's great opus, *Moby Dick*, follows a crazed Captain Ahab on his Homerian odyssey to find and conquer the great white whale that has outwitted him and his whaling crews time and again. The whale has even taken Arab's leg and according to Ahab, wants all of him. Melville recreates in painstaking detail, and with insider knowledge of the harsh life of a whaler out of New Bedford, by way of Nantucket. For those who don't want to learn about every single guy rope or all parts of the whaler's rigging, Melville offers up the succinct tale of Billy Budd and his Christ-like sacrifice to the black and white maritime laws on the high seas. An accident results in the death of one of the ship's officers, a slug of a fellow, who had taken a dislike to the young, affable, shy Billy. Captain Vere must hang Billy for the death of Claggert, but knows that this is not right. However, an example must be given to the rest of the crew so that discipline can be maintained.

Edgar Allan Poe creates a distinctly American version of romanticism with his 16 syllable line in "The Raven," the classical "To Helen," and his Gothic "Annabelle Lee." The horror short story can be said to originate from Poe's pen. "The Tell-Tale Heart," "The Cask of Amontillado," "The Fall of the House of Usher," and "The Masque of the Red Death" are exemplary short stories. The new genre of detective story also emerges with Poe's "Murders in the Rue Morgue."

American Romanticism has its own offshoot in the Transcendentalism of Ralph Waldo Emerson and Henry David Thoreau. One wrote about transcending the complexities of life; the other, who wanted to get to the marrow of life, pitted himself against nature at Walden Pond and wrote an inspiring autobiographical account of his sojourn, aptly titled *On Walden Pond*. He also wrote passionately on his objections to the interference of government on the individual in "On the Duty of Civil Disobedience."

Emerson's elegantly crafted essays and war poetry still give validation to several important universal truths. Probably most remembered for his address to Thoreau's Harvard graduating class, "The American Scholar," he defined the qualities of hard work and intellectual spirit required of Americans in their growing nation.

4. The Transition between Romanticism and Realism

The Civil War period ushers in the poignant poetry of Walt Whitman and his homages to all who suffer from the ripple effects of war and presidential assassination. His "Come up from the Fields, Father" about a Civil War soldier's death and his family's reaction and "When Lilacs Last in the Courtyard Bloom'd" about the effects of Abraham Lincoln's death on the poet and the nation should be required readings in any American literature course. Further, his *Leaves of Grass* gave America its first poetry truly unique in form, structure, and subject matter.

Emily Dickinson, like Walt Whitman, leaves her literary fingerprints on a vast array of poems, all but three of which were never published in her lifetime. Her themes of introspection and attention to nature's details and wonders are, by any measurement, world-class works. Her posthumous recognition reveals the timeliness of her work. American writing had most certainly arrived!

During this period such legendary figures as Paul Bunyan and Pecos Bill rose from the oral tradition. Anonymous storytellers around campfires told tales of a huge lumberman and his giant blue ox, Babe, whose adventures were explanations of natural phenomena like those of footprints filled with rainwater becoming the Great Lakes. Or the whirling dervish speed of Pecos Bill explained the tornadoes of the Southwest. Like ancient peoples, finding reasons for the happenings in their lives, these American pioneer storytellers created a mythology appropriate to the vast reaches of the unsettled frontier.

Mark Twain also left giant footprints with his unique blend of tall tale and fable. "The Celebrated Jumping Frog of Calaveras County" and "The Man who Stole Hadleyburg" are epitomes of short story writing. Move to novel creation, and Twain again rises head and shoulders above others by his bold, still disputed, oft-banned *The Adventures of Huckleberry Finn*, which examines such taboo subjects as a white person's love of a slave, the issue of leaving children with abusive parents, and the outcomes of family feuds. Written partly in dialect and southern vernacular, *The Adventures of Huckleberry Finn* is touted by some as the greatest American novel.

5. The Realistic Period.

The late nineteenth century saw a reaction against the tendency of romantic writers to look at the world through rose-colored glasses. Writers like Frank Norris (*The* Pit) and Upton Sinclair (*The Jungle*) used their novels to decry conditions for workers in slaughterhouses and wheat mills. In *The Red Badge of Courage*, Stephen Crane wrote of the daily sufferings of the common soldier in the Civil War. Realistic writers wrote of common, ordinary people and events using detail that would reveal the harsh realities of life. They broached taboos by creating protagonists whose environments often destroyed them. Romantic writers would have only protagonists whose indomitable wills helped them rise above adversity. Crane's *Maggie: A Girl of the Streets* deals with a young woman forced into prostitution to survive. In "The Occurrence at Owl Creek Bridge," Ambrose Bierce relates the unfortunate hanging of a Confederate soldier.

Upton Sinclair

Short stories, like Bret Harte's "The Outcasts of Poker Flat" and Jack London's "To Build a Fire," deal with unfortunate people whose luck in life has run out. Many writers, sub classified as naturalists, believed that man was subject to a fate over which he had no control.

6. The Modern Era

The twentieth century American writing can be classified into the following three genres.

America Drama

The greatest and most prolific of American playwrights include

Eugene O'Neill -- *Long Day's Journey into Night, Mourning Becomes Electra,* and *Desire Under the Elms*

Arthur Miller -- *The Crucible, All My Sons,* and *Death of a Salesman*

Tennessee Williams -- *Cat on a Hot Tin Roof, The Glass Menagerie,* and *A Street Car Named Desire*

Edward Albee -- *Who's Afraid of Virginia Woolf?, Three Tall Women,* and *A Delicate Balance*

American Fiction

The renowned American novelists of this century include

John Updike -- *Rabbit Run* and *Rabbit Redux*

Sinclair Lewis -- *Babbit* and *Elmer Gantry*

F. Scott Fitzgerald -- *The Great Gatsby* and *Tender is the Night*

Ernest Hemingway -- *A Farewell to Arms* and *For Whom the Bell Tolls*

William Faulkner -- *The Sound and the Fury* and *Absalom, Absalom*

Bernard Malamud -- *The Fixer* and *The Natural*

American Poetry

The poetry of the twentieth century is multifaceted, as represented by Edna St. Vincent Millay, Marianne Moore, Richard Wilbur, Langston Hughes, Maya Angelou, and Rita Lone. Head and shoulders above all others are the many-layered poems of Robert Frost. His New England motifs of snowy evenings, birches, apple picking, stone wall mending, hired hands, and detailed nature studies relate universal truths in exquisite diction, polysyllabic words, and rare allusions to either mythology or the *Bible*.

SKILL 4.4 Identification of fundamental characteristics of major multi-cultural writers including American Indian, Afro-American, Latino/a, and feminist.

American Indian Literature

The foundation of American Indian writing is found in story-telling, oratory, autobiographical and historical accounts of tribal village life, reverence for the environment, and the postulation that the earth with all of its beauty was given in trust, to be cared for and passed on to future generations.

Early American Indian writings

Barland, Hal. *When The Legends Die*

Barrett, S.M. Editor: *Geronimo: His Own Story - Apache*

Eastman, C. & Eastman E. *Wigwam Evenings: Sioux Folktales Retold*

Riggs, L. *Cherokee Night* - drama

20th Century Writers

Deloria, V. *Custer Died for your Sins* (Sioux)

Dorris, M. *The Broken Cord: A Family's on-going struggle with fetal alcohol syndrome* (Modoc)
Hogan, L. *Mean Spirited* (Chickasaw)
Taylor, C.F. *Native American Myths and Legends*

Afro-American Literature

The three phases of Afro-American Literature can be broken down as follows:

- Oppression, slavery, and the re-construction of the post-Civil War/rural South

- Inner city strife/single parenting, drug abuse, lack of educational opportunities and work advancement etc. that was controlled by biased and disinterested factions of society.

- Post-Civil Rights and the emergence of the BLACK movement focusing on biographical and autobiographical Black heroes and their contribution to Black and American culture.

Resources:

1. Pre-Civil War

Bethune, Mary McLoed. *Voice of Black Hope*
Fast, Howard. *Freedom Ride*
Haskins, James. *Black Music in America - A History through its People*
Huggins, Nathan Irving. *Black Odyssey*
Lemann, Nicolas. *The Promised Land*
Stowe, Harriet Beecher. *Uncle Tom's Cabin*
Wheatley, Phyllis. *Memoirs and Poems*

2. Post-Civil War and Reconstruction

Armstrong, William. *Sounder*
Bonham, Frank. *Durango Street*
Childress, Alice. *A Hero Ain't Nothin' But a Sandwich*
Gaines, Ernest. *The Autobiography of Miss Jane Pittman*

3. Post Civil War - Present

Angelou, Maya. *I Know Why the Caged Bird Sings*
Baldwin, James. *Go Tell It on the Mountain*
Haley, Alex. *Roots*
Hansberry, Lorraine. *Raisin in the Sun*
Harper, Lee. *To Kill a Mockingbird*
Hughes, Langston. *I, Too, Sing America*
Wright, Richard. *White Man Listen!* and *Native Son*

Latino/a Literature

In the field of literature, we have two new expanding areas, Latino/a and feminist writers. These authors write to retain cultural heritage, share their people's struggle for recognition, independence, and survival, and express their hopes for the future.

Latino/Latina Writers
De Cervantes, Lora (Chicana). *Starfish*
Cisneros, Sandra (Hispanic). *Red Sweater* and other short story collections
Marquez, Gabriel Garcia (Colombian). *Hundred Years of Solitude*
Nunoz, A. Lopez (Spanish). *Programas Para Dais Especiales*
Neruda, Pablo (Chile). Nobel Prize Winner- Collections of Poetry
Silko, Leslie Marmon (Mexican). *The Time We Climbed Snake Mountain*
Soto, Gary (Mexican). *The Tales of Sunlight*

ENGLISH HIGH SCHOOL

Feminist / gender concern literature written by women in the United States

Edith Wharton's *Ethan Frome* is a heartbreaking tale of lack of communication, lack of funds, the unrelenting cold of the Massachusetts winter, and a toboggan ride which gnarls Ethan and Mattie just like the old tree which they smash into. The *Age of Innocence*, in contrast to *Ethan Frome*, is set in the upper echelons of fin de siècle New York and explores marriage without stifling social protocols.

"I never use it, but I've found it to be a great deterrent."

Willa Cather's work moves the reader to the prairies of Nebraska and the harsh eking out of existence by the immigrant families who choose to stay there and farm. Her most acclaimed works include *My Antonia* and *Death Comes for the Archbishop*.

Kate Chopin's regionalism and local color takes her readers to the upper-crust Creole society of New Orleans and resort isles off the Louisiana coast. "The Story of an Hour" is lauded as one of the greatest of all short stories. Her feminist liberation novel, *The Awakening*, is still hotly debated.

Eudora Welty's regionalism and dialect shine in her short stories of rural Mississippi, especially in "The Worn Path."

Modern black female writers who explore the world of feminist/gender issues as well as class prohibitions are Alice Walker -- (*The Color Purple*), Zora Neale Hurston (*Their Eyes Were Watching God*), and Toni Morrison (*Beloved, Jazz,* and *Song of Solomon*).

Feminists

Alcott, Louisa May. *Little Women*
Friedan, Betty. *The Feminine Mystique: The Second Stage*
Bronte, Charlotte.   *Jane Eyre*
Hurston, Zora Neale. *Their Eyes Were Watching God*
Janeway, Elizabeth. *Woman's World, Woman's Place: A Study in Social Mythology*
Chopin, Kate. *The Awakening*
Rich, Adrienne. Arienne Rich's Poetry: *Motherhood As Experience* and *Driving into the Wreck*
Woolf, Virginia. *A Room of One's Own*

SKILL 4.5 Comprehend the major chronological movements of British literature through acclaimed works by renowned authors in each period.

Anglo-Saxon

The Anglo-Saxon period spans six centuries but produced only a smattering of literature. The first British epic is *Beowulf,* anonymously written by Christian monks many years after the events in the narrative supposedly occurred. This Teutonic saga relates the triumph three times over monsters by the hero, Beowulf. "The Seafarer," a shorter poem, some history, and some riddles are the rest of the Anglo-Saxon canon.

Medieval

The Medieval period introduces Geoffrey Chaucer, the father of English literature, whose *Canterbury Tales* are written in the vernacular, or street language of England, not in Latin. Thus, this famous story is said to be the first work of British literature. Next, Thomas Malory's *Le Morte d'Arthur* calls together the extant tales from Europe as well as England concerning the legendary King Arthur, Merlin, Guenevere, and the Knights of the Round Table. This work is the generative work that gave rise to the many Arthurian legends that stir the chivalric imagination.

Renaissance and Elizabethan

The Renaissance, the most important period since it is synonymous with William Shakespeare, begins with importing the idea of the Petrarchan or Italian sonnet into England. Sir Thomas Wyatt and Sir Philip Sydney wrote English versions. Next, Sir Edmund Spenser invented a variation on this Italian sonnet form, aptly called the Spenserian sonnet. His masterpiece is the epic, *The Fairie Queene*, honoring Queen Elizabeth I's reign. He also wrote books on the Red Cross Knight, St. George and the Dragon, and a series of Arthurian adventures. Spencer was dubbed the Poet's Poet. He created a nine-line stanza, eight lines iambic pentameter and an extra-footed ninth line, an alexandrine. Thus, he invented the Spencerian stanza as well.

William Shakespeare, the Bard of Avon, wrote 154 sonnets, 39 plays, and two long narrative poems. The sonnets are justifiably called the greatest sonnet sequence in all literature. Shakespeare dispensed with the octave/sestet format of the Italian sonnet and invented his three quatrains, one heroic couplet format. His plays are divided into comedies, history plays, and tragedies. Great lines from these plays are more often quoted than from any other author. The Big Four tragedies, Hamlet, *Macbeth*, *Othello*, and *King Lear* are acknowledged to be the most brilliant examples of this genre.

Seventeenth century

John Milton's devout Puritanism was the wellspring of his creative genius that closes the remarkable productivity of the English Renaissance. His social commentary in such works as *Aereopagitica*, *Samson Agonistes*, and his elegant sonnets would be enough to solidify his stature as a great writer. It is his masterpiece based in part on the Book of Genesis that places Milton very near the top of the rung of a handful of the most renowned of all writers. *Paradise Lost*, written in balanced, elegant Neoclassic form, truly does justify the ways of God to man. The greatest allegory about man's journey to the Celestial City (Heaven) was written at the end of the English Renaissance, as was John Bunyan's *The Pilgrim's Progress*, which describes virtues and vices personified. This work is, or was for a long time, second only to the *Bible* in numbers of copies printed and sold.

The Jacobean Age gave us the marvelously witty and cleverly constructed conceits of John Donne's metaphysical sonnets, as well as his insightful meditations, and his version of sermons or homilies. "Ask not for whom the bell tolls", and "No man is an island unto himself" are famous epigrams from Donne's *Meditations*. His most famous conceit is that which compares lovers to a footed compass traveling seemingly separate, but always leaning towards one another and conjoined in "A Valediction Forbidding Mourning."

Eighteenth century

Ben Johnson, author of the wickedly droll play, *Volpone,* and the Cavalier *carpe diem* poets Robert Herrick, Sir John Suckling, and Richard Lovelace also wrote during King James I's reign.

The Restoration and Enlightenment reflect the political turmoil of the regicide of Charles I, the Interregnum Puritan government of Oliver Cromwell, and the restoring of the monarchy to England by the coronation of Charles II, who had been given refuge by the French King Louis. Neoclassicism became the preferred writing style, especially for Alexander Pope. New genres, such as *The Diary of Samuel Pepys*, the novels of Daniel Defoe, the periodical essays and editorials of Joseph Addison and Richard Steele, and Alexander Pope's mock epic, *The Rape of the Lock*, demonstrate the diversity of expression during this time.

Writers who followed were contemporaries of Dr. Samuel Johnson, the lexicographer of *The Dictionary of the English Language*. Fittingly, this Age of Johnson, which encompasses James Boswell's biography of Dr. Johnson, Robert Burns' Scottish dialect and regionalism in his evocative poetry and the mystical pre-Romantic poetry of William Blake usher in the Romantic Age and its revolution against Neoclassicism.

Romantic period

The Romantic Age encompasses what is known as the First Generation Romantics, William Wordsworth and Samuel Taylor Coleridge, who collaborated on *Lyrical Ballads,* which defines and exemplifies the tenets of this style of writing. The Second Generation includes George Gordon, Lord Byron, Percy Bysshe Shelley, and John Keats. These poets wrote sonnets, odes, epics, and narrative poems, most dealing with homage to nature. Wordsworth's most famous other works are "Intimations on Immortality" and "The Prelude." Byron's satirical epic, *Don Juan*, and his autobiographical Childe *Harold's Pilgrimage* are irreverent, witty, self-deprecating and, in part, cuttingly critical of other writers and critics. Shelley's odes and sonnets are remarkable for sensory imagery. Keats' sonnets, odes, and longer narrative poem, *The Eve of St. Agnes*, are remarkable for their introspection and the tender age of the poet, who died when he was only twenty-five. In fact, all of the Second Generation died before their times. Wordsworth, who lived to be eighty, outlived them all, as well as his friend and collaborator, Coleridge. Others who wrote during the Romantic Age are the essayist, Charles Lamb, and the novelist, Jane Austin. The Bronte sisters, Charlotte and Emily, wrote one novel each, which are noted as two of the finest ever written, *Jane Eyre* and *Wuthering* Heights. Marianne Evans, also known as George Eliot, wrote several important novels: her masterpiece, *Middlemarch*, *Silas Marner, Adam Bede,* and *Mill on the Floss*.

Nineteenth century

The Victorian Period is remarkable for the diversity and proliferation of work in three major areas. Poets who are typified as Victorians include Alfred Lord Tennyson, who wrote *Idylls of the King*, twelve narrative poems about the Arthurian legend, and Robert Browning who wrote chilling dramatic monologues, such as "My Last Duchess," as well as long poetic narratives such as *The Pied Piper of Hamlin*. His wife Elizabeth wrote two major works, the epic feminist poem, *Aurora Leigh*, and her deeply moving and provocative *Sonnets* from *the Portuguese* in which she details her deep love for Robert and his startling, to her, reciprocation. Gerard Manley Hopkins, a Catholic priest, wrote poetry with sprung rhythm. (See Glossary of Literary Terms in 4.2). A. E. Housman, Matthew Arnold, and the Pre-Raphaelites, especially the brother and sister duo, Dante Gabriel and Christina Rosetti, contributed much to round out the Victorian Era poetic scene. The Pre-Raphaelites, a group of 19th-century English painters, poets, and critics reacted against Victorian materialism and the neoclassical conventions of academic art by producing earnest, quasi-religious works. Medieval and early Renaissance painters up to the time of the Italian painter Raphael inspired the group. Robert Louis Stevenson, the great Scottish novelist, wrote his adventure/history lessons for young adults. Victorian prose ranges from the incomparable, keenly woven plot structures of Charles Dickens to the deeply moving Dorset/Wessex novels of Thomas Hardy, in which women are repressed and life is more struggle than euphoria. Rudyard Kipling wrote about Colonialism in India in works like *Kim* and *The Jungle Book* that create exotic locales and a distinct main point concerning the Raj, the British Colonial government during Victoria's reign. Victorian drama is mainly a product of Oscar Wilde whose satirical masterpiece, *The Importance of Being Earnest*, farcically details and lampoons Victorian social mores.

Twentieth century

The early twentieth century is mainly represented by the towering achievement of George Bernard Shaw's dramas: *St. Joan, Man and Superman, Major Barbara,* and *Arms and the Man* to name a few. Novelists are too numerous to list, but Joseph Conrad, E. M. Forster, Virginia Woolf, James Joyce, Nadine Gordimer, Graham Greene, George Orwell, and D. H. Lawrence comprise some of the century's very best.

Twentieth century poets of renown and merit include W. H. Auden, Robert Graves, T. S. Eliot, Edith Sitwell, Stephen Spender, Dylan Thomas, Philip Larkin, Ted Hughes, Sylvia Plath, and Hugh MacDarmid. This list is by no means complete.

SKILL 4.6 Distinguish and identify major world writers and their works.

North American Literature

North America is divided into the United States and Canada. The American writers have been amply discussed in 4.3. Canadian writers of note include feminist, Margaret Atwood, (*The Hand Maiden's Tale*); Alice Munro, a remarkable short story writer; and W. P. Kinsella, another short story writer whose two major subjects are North American Indians and baseball.

Central American/Caribbean Literature

The Caribbean and Central America encompass a vast area and cultures that reflect oppression and colonialism by England, Spain, Portugal, France, and The Netherlands. The Caribbean writers include Samuel Selvon from Trinidad and Armado Valladres from Cuba. Central American authors include the novelist, Gabriel Garcia Marquez, (*A Hundred Years of Solitude*) from Columbia, as well as the 1990 Nobel Prize winning poet, Octavia Paz, (*The Labyrinth of Solitude*) from Mexico and feminist Rosarian Castillanos (*The Nine Guardians*), also Mexican. Carlos Solorzano, a dramatist, whose plays include Dona Beatriz, The Hapless, The Magician, and The Hands of God, represents Guatemala.

South American Literature

Chilean Gabriela Mistral was the first Latin American writer to win the Nobel Prize for literature. She is best known for her collections of poetry, *Desolation* and *Feeling*. Chile was also home to Pablo Neruda who, in 1971, also won the Nobel Prize for literature for his poetry. His 29 volumes of poetry have been translated into more than 60 languages attesting to his universal appeal. *Twenty Love Poems* and *Song of Despair* are justly famous. Isabel Allende is carrying on the Chilean literary standards with her acclaimed novel, *House of Spirits*.
Argentinean Jorge Luis Borges is considered by many literary critics to be the most important writer of this century from South America. His collections of short stories, *Ficciones*, brought him universal recognition. Also from Argentina, Silvina Ocampo, a collaborator with Borges on a collection of poetry, is famed for her poetry and short story collections, which include *The Fury* and *The Days of the Night*.

Noncontinental European Literature

Horacio Quiroga represents Uruguay, and Brazil has Joao Guimaraes Rosa, whose novel, *The Devil to Pay*, is considered first rank world literature.

Continental European Literature

This category excludes British Literature, since the entire section 4.5 deals with writings from Scotland, Ireland, Wales and England.

Germany

German poet and playwright, Friedrich von Schiller, is best known for his history plays, *William Tell* and *The Maid of Orleans*. He is a leading literary figure in Germany's Golden Age of Literature. Also from Germany, Rainer Maria Rilke, the great lyric poet, is one of the poets of the unconscious, or stream of consciousness. Germany also has given the world Herman Hesse, (*Siddartha*), Gunter Grass (*The Tin Drum*), and the greatest of all German writers, Goethe.

Scandinavia

Scandinavia has encouraged the work of Hans Christian Andersen in Denmark who advanced the fairy tale genre with such wistful tales as "The Little Mermaid" and "Thumbelina." The social commentary of Henrik Ibsen in Norway startled the world of drama with such issues as feminism (*The Doll's House* and *Hedda Gabler*) and the effects of sexually transmitted diseases (The Wild Duck and *Ghosts*). Sweden's Selma Lagerlof is the first woman to ever win the Nobel Prize for literature. Her novels include *Gosta Berling's Saga* and the world-renowned *The Wonderful Adventures of Nils*, a children's work.

Russia

Russian literature is vast and monumental. Who has not heard of Fyodor Dostoyevski, or Count Leo Tolstoy's *Crime and Punishment, The Idiot,* and *The Brothers Karamazov*? These are examples of psychological realism. Dostoyevski's influence on modern writers cannot be overly stressed. Tolstoy's *War and Peace* is the sweeping account of the invasion of Russia and Napoleon's taking of Moscow, abandoned by the Russians. This novel is called the national novel of Russia. Further advancing Tolstoy's greatness is his ability to create believable, unforgettable female characters, especially Natasha in *War and Peace* and the heroine of *Anna Karenina* . Puskin is famous for great short stories; Anton Chekhov for drama, (*Uncle Vanya, The Three Sisters, The Cherry Orchard*); Yvteshenko for poetry (*Babi Yar*). Boris Pasternak won the Nobel Prize (*Dr. Zhivago*). Aleksandr Solzhenitsyn (*The Gulag Archipelago*) is only recently back in Russia after years of expatriation in Vermont. Ilya Varshavsky who creates fictional societies that are dystopias, or the opposite of utopias, represents the genre of science fiction.

France

France has a multifaceted canon of great literature that is universal in scope, almost always championing some social cause: the poignant short stories of Guy de Maupassant; the fantastic poetry of Charles Baudelaire (*Fleurs de Mal*); the groundbreaking lyrical poetry of Rimbaud and Verlaine; and the existentialism of Jean-Paul Sartre (*No Exit, The Flies, Nausea*), Andre Malraux, (*The Fall*), and Albert Camus (*The Stranger, The Plague*), the 1957 Nobel Prize for literature recipient. Drama in France is best represented by Rostand's *Cyrano de Bergerac*, and the neo-classical dramas of Racine and Corneille (*El Cid*). Feminist writings include those of Sidonie-Gabrielle Colette known for her short stories and novels, as well as Simone de Beauvoir. The great French novelists include Andre Gide, Honore de Balzac (*Cousin Bette*), Stendel (*The Red and the Black*), the father/son duo of Alexandre Dumas (*The Three Musketeers* and *The Man in the Iron Mask*. Victor Hugo is the Charles Dickens of French literature having penned the masterpieces, *The Hunchback of Notre Dame* and the French national novel, *Les Miserables*. The stream of consciousness of Proust's *Remembrance of Things Past*, and the Absurdist theatre of Samuel Beckett and Eugene Ianesco (*The Rhinoceros*) attest to the groundbreaking genius of the French writers.

Slavic nations

Austrian writer Franz Kafka (*The Metamorphosis, The Trial,* and *The Castle*) is considered by many to be the literary voice of the first-half of the twentieth century. Representing the Czech Republic is the poet Vaclav Havel. Slovakia has dramatist Karel Capek (*R.U.R*). Romania is represented by Elie Weisel (*Night*), a Nobel Prize winner.

Spain

Spain's great writers include Miguel de Cervantes (*Don Quixote*) and Juan Ramon Jimenez. The anonymous national epic, *El Cid*, has been translated into many languages.

Italy

Italy's greatest writers include Virgil, who wrote the great epic (The Aeneid); Giovanni Boccaccio (*The Decameron*); Dante Alighieri (*The Divine Comedy*); and Alberto Moravia.

Ancient Greece

Greece will always be foremost in literary assessments due to its Homer's epics, *The Iliad* and *The Odyssey*. No one, except Shakespeare, is more often cited. Add to these the works of Plato and Aristotle for philosophy; the dramatists Aeschylus, Euripides, and Sophocles for tragedy, and Aristophanes for comedy. Greece is not only the cradle of democracy, but of literature as well.

Africa

African literary greats include South Africans Nadine Gordimer (Nobel Prize for literature) and Peter Abrahams (*Tell Freedom: Memories of Africa*), an autobiography of life in Johannesburg. Chinua Achebe (*Things Fall Apart*) and the poet, Wole Soyinka, hail from Nigeria. Mark Mathabane wrote an autobiography *Kaffir Boy* about growing up in South Africa. Egyptian writer, Naguib Mahfouz, and Doris Lessing from Rhodesia, now Zimbabwe, write about race relations in their respective countries. Because of her radical politics, Lessing was banned from her homeland and The Union of South Africa, as was Alan Paton whose seemingly simple story, *Cry, the Beloved Country*, brought the plight of blacks and the whites' fear of blacks under apartheid to the rest of the world.

Far East

Asia has many modern writers who are being translated for the western reading public. India's Krishan Chandar has authored more than 300 stories. Rabindranath Tagore won the Nobel Prize for literature in 1913 (*Song Offerings*). Narayan, India's most famous writer (*The Guide*), is highly interested in mythology and legends of India. Santha Rama Rau's work, *Gifts of Passage*, is her true story of life in a British school where she tries to preserve her Indian culture and traditional home.

Revered as Japan's most famous female author, Fumiko Hayashi (*Drifting Clouds*) by the time of her death had written more than 270 literary works. The classical Age of Japanese literary achievement includes the father Kiyotsugu Kan ami and the son Motokkiyo Zeami who developed the theatrical experience known as No drama to its highest aesthetic degree. The son is said to have authored over 200 plays, of which 100 still are extant.

In 1968 the Nobel Prize for literature was awarded to Yasunari Kawabata (*The Sound of the Mountain, The Snow Country*) considered to be his masterpieces. His Palm-of-the-Hand Stories take the essentials of Haiku poetry and transform them into the short story genre.

Katai Tayama (*The Quilt*) is touted as the father of the genre known as the Japanese confessional novel. He also wrote in the "ism" of naturalism. His works are definitely not for the squeamish.

The "slice of life" psychological writings of Ryunosuke Akutagawa gained him acclaim in the western world. His short stories, especially "Rashamon" and "In a Grove," are greatly praised for style as well as content.

China, too, has given to the literary world. Li Po, the T'ang dynasty poet from the Chinese Golden Age, revealed his interest in folklore by preserving the folk songs and mythology of China. Po further allows his reader to enter into the Chinese philosophy of Taoism and to know this feeling against expansionism during the T'ang dynastic rule. Back to the T'ang dynasty, which was one of great diversity in the arts, the Chinese version of a short story was created with the help of Jiang Fang. His themes often express love between a man and a woman. Modern feminist and political concerns are written eloquently by Ting Ling, who used the pseudonym Chiang Ping-Chih. Her stories reflect her concerns about social injustice and her commitment to the women's movement.

SKILL 4.7 Demonstrate knowledge of adolescent literature and its relationship to adolescent development.

Prior to twentieth century research on child development and child/adolescent literature's relationship to that development, books for adolescents were primarily didactic. They were designed to be instructive of history, manners, and morals.

Middle Ages

As early as the eleventh century, Anselm, the Archbishop of Canterbury, wrote an encyclopedia designed to instill in children the beliefs and principles of conduct acceptable to adults in medieval society. Early monastic translations of the *Bible* and other religious writings were written in Latin, for the edification of the upper class. Fifteenth century hornbooks were designed to teach reading and religious lessons. William Caxton printed English versions of *Aesop's Fables*, Malory's *Le Morte d'Arthur* and stories from Greek and Roman mythology. Though printed for adults, tales of adventures of Odysseus and the Arthurian knights were also popular with literate adolescents.

Renaissance

The Renaissance saw the introduction of the inexpensive chapbooks, small in size and 16-64 pages in length. Chapbooks were condensed versions of mythology and fairy tales. Designed for the common people, chapbooks were imperfect grammatically but were immensely popular because of their adventurous contents. Though most of the serious, educated adults frowned on the sometimes vulgar little books, they received praise from Richard Steele of *Tatler* fame for inspiring his grandson's interest in reading and pursuing his other studies.

Meanwhile, the Puritans' three most popular reads were the *Bible*, John Foxe's *Book of Martyrs*, and John Bunyan's *Pilgrim's Progress*. Though venerating religious martyrs and preaching the moral propriety which was to lead to eternal happiness, the stories of the *Book of Martyrs* were often lurid in their descriptions of the fate of the damned. Not written for children and difficult reading even for adults, *Pilgrim's Progress* was as attractive to adolescents for its adventurous plot as for its moral outcome. In Puritan America, the *New England Primer* set forth the prayers, catechisms, *Bible* verses, and illustrations meant to instruct children in the Puritan ethic. The seventeenth century French used fables and fairy tales to entertain adults, but children found them enjoyable as well.

Seventeenth century

The late seventeenth century brought the first concern with providing literature that specifically targeted the young. Pierre Perrault's *Fairy Tales*, Jean de la Fontaine's retellings of famous fables, Mme. d'Aulnoy's novels based on old folktales, and Mme. de Beaumont's "Beauty and the Beast" were written to delight as well as instruct young people. In England, publisher John Newbury was the first to publish a line for children. These include a translation of Perrault's *Tales of Mother Goose; A Little Pretty Pocket-Book*, "intended for instruction and amusement" but decidedly moralistic and bland in comparison to the previous century's chapbooks; and *The Renowned History of Little Goody Two Shoes*, allegedly written by Oliver Goldsmith for a juvenile audience.

Eighteenth century

By and large, however, into the eighteenth century adolescents were finding their reading pleasure in adult books: Daniel Defoe's *Robinson Crusoe*, Jonathan Swift's *Gulliver's Travels*, and Johann Wyss's *Swiss Family Robinson*. More books were being written for children, but the moral didacticism, though less religious, was nevertheless ever present. The short stories of Maria Edgeworth, the four volume *The History of Sandford and Merton* by Thomas Day, and Martha Farquharson's twenty-six volume *Elsie Dinsmore* series dealt with pious protagonists who learned restraint, repentance, and rehabilitation from sin. Two bright spots in this period of didacticism were Jean Jacques Rousseau's *Emile* and *The Tales of Shakespear*, Charles and Mary Lamb's simplified versions of Shakespeare's plays. Rousseau believed that a child's abilities were enhanced by a free happy life, and the Lambs subscribed to the notion that children were entitled to more entertaining literature in language comprehensible to their reading ability.

Nineteenth century

Child/adolescent literature truly began its modern rise in nineteenth century Europe. Hans Christian Andersen's *Fairy Tales* were fanciful adaptations of the somber revisions of the Grimm brothers in the previous century. Andrew Lang's series of colorful fairy books contain the folklores of many nations and are still part of the collections of many modern libraries. Clement Moore's "A Visit from St. Nicholas" is a cheery, non-threatening child's view of the "night before Christmas." The humor of Lewis Carroll's books about Alice's adventures, Edward Lear's poems with caricatures, Lucretia Nole's stories of the Philadelphia Peterkin family were full of fancy and not a smidgen of morality. Other popular Victorian novels introduced the modern fantasy and science fiction genres: William Makepeace Thackeray's *The Rose and the Ring*, Charles Dickens' *The Magic Fishbone*, and Jules Verne's *Twenty Thousand Leagues Under the Sea*. Adventure to exotic places became a popular topic: Rudyard Kipling's *Jungle Books*, Verne's *Around the World in Eighty Days*, and Robert Louis Stevenson's *Treasure Island* and *Kidnapped*. In 1884, the first English translation Johanna Spyre's *Heidi* appeared.

North America was also finding its voices for adolescent readers. American Louisa May Alcott's *Little Women* and Canadian L.M. Montgomery's *Anne of Green Gables* ushered in the modern age of realistic fiction. American youth were enjoying the articles of Tom Sawyer and Huckleberry Finn. For the first time children were able to read books about real people just like themselves.

Twentieth century

The literature of the twentieth century is extensive and diverse, and as in previous centuries much influenced by the adults who write, edit, and select books for youth consumption. In the first third of the century, suitable adolescent literature dealt with children from good homes with large families. These books projected an image of a peaceful, rural existence. Though the characters and plots were more realistic, the stories maintained focus on topics that were considered emotionally and intellectually proper. Popular at this time were Laura Ingalls Wilder's Little House on the Prairie Series and Carl Sandburg's biography *Abe Lincoln Grows Up*. English author J.R.R. Tolkein's fantasy *The Hobbit* prefaced modern adolescent readers' fascination with the works of Piers Antony, Madelaine L'Engle, and Anne McCaffery.

Adolescent Development

The social changes of post-World War II significantly affected adolescent literature. The Civil Rights movement, feminism, the protest of the Viet Nam Conflict, and issues surrounding homelessness, neglect, teen pregnancy, drugs, and violence have bred a new vein of contemporary fiction that helps adolescents understand and cope with the world they live in.

Popular books for preadolescents deal more with establishing relationships with members of the opposite sex (Sweet Valley High series) and learning to cope with their changing bodies, personalities, or life situations as in Judy Blume's *Are You There, God? It's Me, Margaret*. Adolescents are still interested in the fantasy and science fiction genres as well as the popular juvenile fiction. Middle school students still read the Little House on the Prairie series and the mysteries of the Hardy boys and Nancy Drew. Teens value the works of Emily and Charlotte Bronte, Willa Cather, Jack London, William Shakespeare, and Mark Twain as much as those of Piers Anthony, S.E. Hinton, Madeleine L'Engle, Stephen King, and J.R.R. Tolkein because they're fun to read whatever their underlying worth may be.

Older adolescents enjoy the writers in these genres.

1. Fantasy: Piers Anthony, Ursula LeGuin, Ann McCaffrey

2. Horror: V.C. Andrews, Stephen King

3. Juvenile fiction: Judy Blume, Robert Cormier, Rosa Guy, Virginia Hamilton, S.E. Hinton, M.E. Kerr, Harry Mazer, Norma Fox Mazer, Richard Newton Peck, Cynthia Voight, and Paul Zindel.

4. Science fiction: Isaac Asimov, Ray Bradbury, Arthur C. Clarke, Frank Herbert, Larry Niven, H.G. Wells.

Child Development Theories Influence on Literature

The late nineteenth and early twentieth centuries' studies by behaviorists and developmental psychologists significantly affected the manner in which the education community and parents approached the selection of literature for children.

The cognitive development studies of Piaget, the epigenetic view of personality development by Erik Erikson, the formulation of Abraham Maslow's hierarchy of basic needs, and the social learning theory of behaviorists like Alfred Bandura contributed to a greater understanding of child/adolescent development even as these theorists contradicted each others findings. Though few educators today totally subscribe to Piaget's inflexible stages of mental development, his principles of both qualitative and quantitative mental capacity, his generalizations about the parallels between physical growth and thinking capacity, and his support of the adolescent's heightened moral perspective are still used as measures by which to evaluate child/adolescent literature.

Piaget's four stages of mental development:

- Sensimotor intelligence (birth to age two) deals with the pre-language period of development. The child is most concerned with coordinating movement and action. Words begin to represent people and things.

- Preoperational thought is the period spanning ages 2-12. It is broken into several substages.

    1. Preconceptual (2-4) phase - most behavior is based on subjective judgment.

    2. Intuitive (4-7) phase - children use language to verbalize their experiences and mental processes.

- Concrete operations (7-11) - children begin to apply logic to concrete things and experiences. They can combine performance and reasoning to solve problems.

- Formal operations (12-15) - adolescents begin to think beyond the immediate and to theorize. They apply formal logic to interpreting abstract constructions and to recognizing experiences that are contrary to fact.

Though Piaget presented these stages as progressing sequentially, a given child might enter any period earlier or later than most children. Furthermore, a child might perform at different levels in different situations. Thus, a fourteen year old female might be able to function at the formal operations stage in a literature class, but function at a concrete operations level in mathematical concepts.

Piaget's Theories Influence Literature

Most middle school students have reached the concrete operations level. By this time they have left behind their egocentrism for a need to understand the physical and social world around them. They become more interested in ways to relate to other people. Their favorite stories become those about real people rather than animals or fairy tale characters. The conflicts in their literature are internal as well as external. Books like Paula Fox's *The Stone-Faced Boy*, Betsy Byards' *The Midnight Fox*, and Lois Lenski's *Strawberry Girl* deal with a child's loneliness, confusion about identity or loyalty, and poverty. Pre-adolescents are becoming more cognizant of and interested in the past, thus their love of adventure stories about national heroes like Davy Crockett, Daniel Boone, and Abe Lincoln and biographies/autobiographies of real life heroes, like Jackie

Robinson and Cesar Chevas. At this level, children also become interested in the future; thus, their love of both fantasy (most medieval in spirit) and science fiction.

The seven to eleven year olds also internalize moral values. They are concerned with their sense of self and are willing to question rules and adult authority. In books such as Beverly Cleary's *Henry Huggins* and *Mitch and Amy*, the protagonists are children pursuing their own desires with the same frustrations as other children. When these books were written in the 1960s, returning a found pet or overcoming a reading disability were common problems.

From twelve to fifteen, adolescents advance beyond the concrete operations level to begin developing communication skills that enable them to articulate attitudes/opinions and exchange knowledge. They can recognize and contrast historical fiction from pure history and biography. They can identify the elements of literature and their relationships within a specific story. As their thinking becomes more complex, early adolescents become more sensitive to others' emotions and reactions. They become better able to suspend their disbelief and enter the world of literature, thus expanding their perceptions of the real world.

In discussing the adolescent's moral judgment, Piaget noted that after age eleven, children stopped viewing actions as either "right" or "wrong." The older child considers both the intent and the behavior in its context. A younger child would view an accidental destruction of property in terms of the amount of damage. The older child would find the accident less wrong than minor damage done with intended malice.

Kohlberg's Theories of Moral Development

Expanding on Piaget's thinking, Lawrence Kohlberg developed a hierarchy of values. Though progressive, the stages of Kohlberg's hierarchy are not clearly aligned to chronological age. The six stages of development correlate to three levels of moral judgment.

Level I. Moral values reside in external acts rather than in persons or standards.

Stage 0. Premoral - No association of actions or needs with sense of right or wrong.

Stage 1. Obedience and punishment orientation. Child defers to adult authority. His actions are motivated by a desire to stay out of trouble.

Stage 2. Right action/self-interest orientation. Performance of right deeds results in needing satisfaction.

Level II. Moral values reside in maintaining conventions of right behavior.

> Stage 3. Good person orientation. The child performs right actions to receive approval from others, conforming to the same standards.
>
> Stage 4. Law and order orientation. Doing one's duty and showing respect for authority contributes to maintaining social order.

Level III. Moral values reside in principles separate in association from the persons or agencies that enforce these principles.

> Stage 5. Legalistic orientation. The rules of society are accepted as correct but alterable. Privileges and duties are derived from social contact. Obedience to society's rules protects the rights of self and others.
>
> Stage 6. Conscience orientation. Ethical standards, such as justice, equality, and respect for others, guide moral conduct more than legal rules.

Though these stages represent a natural progression of values to actions relationships, persons may regress to an earlier stage in certain situations. An adolescent already operating at Stage 5 may regress to Stage 3 in a classroom where consequences of non-conformity are met with disapproval or punishment. An adult operating at Stage 6 may regress to Stage 4 when obligated by military training or confronted with a conflict between self-preservation and the protection of others.

Values clarification education based on Piaget's and Kohlberg's theories imply that development is inherent in human socialization. Becoming a decent person is a natural result of human development.

Social Learning Theory

Much of traditional learning theory resulted from the work of early behaviorists, like B. F. Skinner, and has been refined by modern theorists such as Albert Bandura. Behaviorists believe that intellectual, and therefore behavioral, development cannot be divided into specific stages. They believe that behavior is the result of conditioning experiences, a continuum of rewards and punishments. Environmental conditions are viewed as greater stimuli than inherent qualities. Thus in social learning theory the consequences of behavior - that is, the rewards or punishments - are more significant in social development than are the motivations for the behavior.

Bandura also proposed that a child learns vicariously through observing the behavior of others, whereas the developmental psychologists presumed that children developed through the actual self-experience.

The Humanistic Theory of Development

No discussion of child development would be complete without a review of Abraham Maslow's hierarchy of needs, from basic physiological needs to the need for self-actualization. The following list represents those needs from the hierarchy that most affect children.

1. **Need for physical well-being.** In young children the provisions for shelter, food, clothing, and protection by significant adults satisfy this need. In older children, this satisfaction of physical comforts translates to a need for material security and may manifest itself in struggles to overcome poverty and maintain the integrity of home and family.

2. **Need for love.** The presumption is that every human being needs to love and be loved. With young children this reciprocal need is directed at and received from parents and other family members, pets, and friends. In older children and adolescents this need for love forms the basis for romance and peer acceptance.

3. **Need to belong.** Beyond the need for one-on-one relationships, a child needs the security of being an accepted member of a group. Young children identify with family, friends, and schoolmates. They are concerned with having happy experiences and being accepted by people they love and respect. Later, they associate with community, country, and perhaps world groups. Adolescents become more aware of a larger world order and thus develop concerns about issues facing society, such as political or social unrest, wars, discrimination, and environmental issues. They seek to establish themselves with groups who accept and share their values. They become more team oriented.

4. **Need to achieve competence.** A human's need to interact satisfactorily with his environment begins with the infant's exploration of his immediate surroundings. Visual and tactile identification of objects and persons provides confidence to perform further explorations. To become well adjusted, the child must achieve competence to feel satisfaction. Physical and intellectual achievements become measures of acceptance. Frustrations resulting from physical or mental handicaps are viewed as hurtles to be overcome if satisfaction is to be achieved. Older children view the courage-overcome obstacles as part of the maturing process.

5. **Need to know.** Curiosity is the basis of intelligence. The need to learn is persistent. To maintain intellectual security, children must be able to find answers to their questions in order to stimulate further exploration of information to satisfy that persistent curiosity.

6. **Need for beauty and order.** Aesthetic satisfaction is as important as the need for factual information. Intellectual stimulation comes from satisfying curiosity about the fine, as well as the practical, arts. Acceptance for one's accomplishments in dance, music, drawing, writing, or performing/ appreciating any of the arts leads to a sense of accomplishment and self-actualization.

Theory of Psychosocial Development

Erik Erikson, a follower of Sigmund Freud, presented the theory that human development consists of maturation through as series of psychosocial crisis. The struggle to resolve these crises helps a person achieve individuality as he learns to function in society.

Maturation occurs as the individual moves through a progression of increasingly complex stages. The movement from one stage to the next hinges on the successful resolution of the conflicts encountered in each stage, and each of the stages represents a step in identity formation. Stage 1 (trust versus distrust), stage 2 (achieving autonomy), and stage 3 (developing initiative) relate to infants and young/middle children. Stages 4 and 5 relate to late childhood through adolescents.

Stage 4 - **Becoming Industrious.** Late childhood, according to Erikson, occurs between seven to eleven. Having already mastered conflicts that helped them overcome mistrust of unfamiliar persons, places, and things; that made them more independent in caring for themselves and their possessions; and that overcame their sense of guilt at behavior that creates opposition with others, children are ready to assert themselves in suppressing feelings of inferiority. Children at this stage learn to master independent tasks as well as to work cooperatively with other children. They increasingly measure their own competence by comparing themselves to their peers.

Stage 5 - **Establishing Identity**. From age eleven through the teen years, a person's conflicts arise from his search for identity, as an individual and a member of society. Because internal demands for independence and peer acceptance sometimes oppose external demands for conformity to rules and standards, friction with family, school, and society in general occur during these years. The adolescent must resolve issues such as the amount of control he will concede to family and other rule enforcing adults as he searches for other acceptance models. In his quest for self-identity, he experiments with adult behavior and attitudes. At the end of his teen years, he should have a well - established sense of identity.

Theory of multiple intelligences

Howard Gardner's research in the 1980s has been recently influential in helping teachers understand that human beings process information differently and, therefore, communicate their knowledge through different modes of operation. It is important to present language and literature in visual, auditory, tactile, and kinesthetic ways to allow every child to develop good skills through his own mode of learning. Then, the child himself must be allowed to perform through the strength of his intelligence. The movement toward learning academies in the practical and fine arts and in the sciences is a result of our growing understanding of all aspects of child development.

Modern society's role in child development

Despite their differences, there are many similarities in the theories of child development. However, most of these theories were developed prior to the social unrest of the 1970s. In industrialized Western society, children are increasingly excluded from the activities of work and play with adults and education has become their main occupation. This exclusion tends to prolong childhood and adolescents and thus inhibit development as visualized by theorists. For adolescents in America, this prolonging results in slower social and intellectual maturation, contrasted to increasing physical maturity. Adolescents today deal with drugs, violence, communicable diseases, and a host of social problems that were of minimal concerns thirty years ago. Even pre-adolescent children are dealing with poverty, disease, broken homes, abuse, and drugs.

Influence of Theories on Literature

All of these development theories and existing social conditions influence the literature created and selected for and by child/adolescent readers.

Child/adolescent literature has always been to some degree didactic, whether non-fiction or fiction. Until the twentieth century, "kiddie" lit was also morally prescriptive. Written by adults who determined either what they believed children needed or liked or what they should need or like, most books, stories, poems, and essays dealt with experiences or issues that would make children into better adults. The fables, fairy tales, and epics of old set the moral/social standards of their times while entertaining the child in every reader/listener. These tales are still popular because they have a universal appeal. Except for the rare exceptions discussed earlier in this section, most books were written for literate adults. Educated children found their pleasure in the literature that was available.

Benefits of research

One benefit of the child development and learning theory research is that they provide guidelines for writers, publishers, and educators to follow in the creation, marketing, and selection of good reading materials. MacMillan introduced children's literature as a separate publishing market in 1918. By the 1930s, most major publishers had a children's department. Though arguments have existed throughout this century about quality versus quantity, there is no doubt that children's literature is a significant slice of the market pie.

Another influence is that children's books are a reflection of both developmental theories and social changes. Reading provides children with the opportunity to become more aware of societal differences, to measure their behavior against the behavior of realistic fictional characters or the subjects of biographies, to become informed about events of the past and present that will affect their futures, and to acquire a genuine appreciation of literature.

Furthermore, there is an obligation for adults to provide instruction and entertainment that all children in our democratic society can use. As parents and educators we have a further obligation to guide children in the selection of books that are appropriate to their reading ability and interest levels. Of course, there is a fine line between guidance and censorship. As with discipline, parents learn that to make forbidden is to make more desirable. To publish a list of banned books is to make them suddenly attractive. Most children/adolescents left to their own selections will choose books on topics that interest them and are written in language they can understand.

Impact of research on teachers

Adolescent literature, because of the age range of readers, is extremely diverse. Fiction for the middle group, usually ages ten/eleven to fourteen/fifteen, deals with issues of coping with internal and external changes in their lives. Because children's writers in the twentieth century have produced increasingly realistic fiction, adolescents can now find problems dealt with honestly in novels.

Teachers of middle/junior high school students see the greatest change in interests and reading abilities. Fifth and sixth graders, included in elementary grades in many schools, are viewed as older children while seventh and eighth graders are preadolescent. Ninth graders, included sometimes as top dogs in junior high school and sometimes as underlings in high school, definitely view themselves as teenagers. Their literature choices will often be governed more by interest than by ability; thus, the wealth of high-interest, low readability books that have flooded the market in recent years. Tenth through twelfth graders will still select high-interest books for pleasure reading but are also easily encouraged to stretch their literature muscles by reading more classics.

Because of the rapid social changes, topics that once did not interest young people until they reached their teens - suicide, gangs, homosexuality - are now subjects of books for even younger readers. The plethora of high-interest books reveals how desperately schools have failed to produce on-level readers and how the market has adapted to that need. However, these high-interest books are now readable for younger children whose reading levels are at or above normal. No matter how tastefully written, some contents are inappropriate for younger readers. The problem becomes not so much steering them toward books that they have the reading ability to handle but encouraging them toward books whose content is appropriate to their levels of cognitive and social development. A fifth-grader may be able to read V.C. Andrews book *Flowers in the Attic* but not possess the social/moral development to handle the deviant behavior of the characters. At the same time, because of the complex changes affecting adolescents, the teacher must be well versed in learning theory and child development as well as competent to teach the subject matter of language and literature.

Popular literature related to learning development theories

For fifth and sixth grade

These classic and contemporary works combine the characteristics of multiple theories. Functioning at the concrete operations stage (Piaget), being of the "good person," orientation (Kohlberg), still highly dependent on external rewards (Bandura), and exhibiting all five needs previously discussed from Maslow's hierarchy, these eleven to twelve year olds should appreciate the following titles, grouped by reading level. These titles are also cited for interest at that grade level and do not reflect high-interest titles for older readers who do not read at grade level. Some high interest titles will be cited later.

Reading level 6.0 to 6.9

Barrett, William. *Lilies of the Field*
Cormier, Robert. *Other Bells for Us to Ring*
Dahl, Roald. *Danny, Champion of the World; Charlie and the Chocolate Factory*
Lindgren, Astrid. *Pippi Longstocking*
Lindbergh, Anne. *Three Lives to Live*
Lowry, Lois. *Rabble Starkey*
Naylor, Phyllis. *The Year of the Gopher, Reluctantly Alice*
Peck, Robert Newton. *Arly*
Speare, Elizabeth. *The Witch of Blackbird Pond*
Sleator, William. *The Boy Who Reversed Himself*

For seventh and eighth grades

Most seventh and eight grade students, according to learning theory, are still functioning cognitively, psychologically, and morally as sixth graders. As these are not inflexible standards, there are some twelve and thirteen year olds who are much more mature socially, intellectually, and physically than the younger children who share the same school. They are becoming concerned with establishing individual and peer group identities that presents conflicts with breaking from authority and the rigidity of rules. Some at this age are still tied firmly to the family and its expectations while others identify more with those their own age or older. Enrichment reading for this group must help them cope with life's rapid changes or provide escape and thus must be either realistic or fantastic depending on the child's needs. Adventures and mysteries (the Hardy Boys and Nancy Drew series) are still popular today. These preteens also become more interested in biographies of contemporary figures rather than legendary figures of the past.

Reading level 7.0 to 7.9

Armstrong, William. *Sounder*
Bagnold, Enid. *National Velvet*
Barrie, James. *Peter Pan*
London, Jack. *White Fang, Call of the Wild*
Lowry, Lois. *Taking Care of Terrific*
McCaffrey, Anne. The *Dragonsinger* series
Montgomery, L. M. *Anne of Green Gables* and sequels
Steinbeck, John. *The Pearl*
Tolkien, J. R. R. *The Hobbit*
Zindel, Paul. *The Pigman*

Reading level 8.0 to 8.9

Cormier, Robert. *I Am the Cheese*
McCullers, Carson. *The Member of the Wedding*
North, Sterling. *Rascal*
Twain, Mark. *The Adventures of Tom Sawyer*
Zindel, Paul. *My Darling , My Hamburger*

For ninth grade

Depending upon the school environment, a ninth grader may be top-dog in a junior high school or underdog in a high school. Much of his social development and thus his reading interests become motivated by his peer associations. He is technically an adolescent operating at the early stages of formal operations in cognitive development. His perception of his own identity is becoming well-defined and he is fully aware of the ethics required by society. He is more receptive to the challenges of classic literature but still enjoys popular teen novels.

Reading level 9.0 to 9.9

Brown, Dee. *Bury My Heart at Wounded Knee*
Defoe, Daniel. *Robinson Crusoe*
Dickens, Charles. *David Copperfield*
Greenberg, Joanne. *I Never Promised You a Rose Garden*
Kipling, Rudyard. *Captains Courageous*
Mathabane, Mark. *Kaffir Boy*
Nordhoff, Charles. *Mutiny on the Bounty*
Shelley, Mary. *Frankenstein*
Washington, Booker T. *Up From Slavery*

For tenth - twelfth grades

All high school sophomores, juniors and seniors can handle most other literature except for a few of the very most difficult titles like *Moby Dick* or *Vanity Fair*. However, since many high school students do not progress to the eleventh or twelfth grade reading level, they will still have their favorites among authors whose writings they can understand. Many will struggle with assigned novels but still read high interest books for pleasure. A few high interest titles are listed below without reading level designations, though most are 6.0 to 7.9.

> Bauer, Joan. *Squashed*
> Borland, Hal. *When the Legends Die*
> Danzinger, Paula. *Remember Me to Herald Square*
> Duncan, Lois. *Stranger with my Face*
> Hamilton, Virginia. *The Planet of Junior Brown*
> Hinton, S. E. *The Outsiders*
> Paterson, Katherine. *The Great Gilly Hopkins*

Teachers of students at all levels must be familiar with the materials offered by the libraries in their own schools. Only then can she guide her students into appropriate selections for their social age and reading level development.

SKILL 4.8 Identify elements of literature from which allusions are drawn.

Literary allusions are drawn from classic mythology, national folklore, and religious writings that are supposed to have such familiarity to the reader that he can recognize the comparison between the subject of the allusion and the person, place, or event in the current reading. Children and adolescents who have knowledge of proverbs, fables, myths, epics, and the *Bible* can understand these allusions and thereby appreciate their reading to a greater degree than those who cannot recognize them.

Fables and folktales

This literary group of stories and legends was originally orally transmitted to the common populace to provide models of exemplary behavior or deeds worthy of recognition and homage.

In fables, animals talk, feel, and behave like human beings. The fable always has a moral and the animals illustrate specific people or groups without directly identifying them. For example, in Aesop's *Fables*, the lion is the "King" and the wolf is the cruel, often unfeeling, "noble class." In the fable of "The Lion and the Mouse" the moral is that "Little friends may prove to be great friends." In "The Lion's Share" it is "Might makes right." Many British folktales - *How Robin*

Became an Outlaw and *St. George - Slaying of the Dragon* - stress the correlation between power and right.

Classical mythology

Much of the mythology that produces allusions in modern English writings is a product of ancient Greece and Rome because these myths have been more liberally translated. Some Norse myths are also well known. Children are fond of myths because those ancient people were seeking explanations for those elements in their lives that predated scientific knowledge just as children seek explanations for the occurrences in their lives. These stories provide insight into the order and ethics of life as ancient heroes overcome the terrors of the unknown and bring meaning to the thunder and lightning, to the changing of the seasons, to the magical creatures of the forests and seas, and to the myriad of natural phenomena that can frighten mankind. There is often a childlike quality in the emotions of supernatural beings with which children can identify. Many good translations of myths exist for readers of varying abilities, but Edith Hamilton's *Mythology* is the most definitive reading for adolescents.

Fairy tales

Fairy tales are lively fictional stories involving children or animals that come in contact with super-beings via magic. They provide happy solutions to human dilemmas. The fairy tales of many nations are peopled by trolls, elves, dwarfs, and pixies, child-sized beings capable of fantastic accomplishments.

Among the most famous are "Beauty and the Beast," " Cinderella," " Hansel and Gretel," " Snow White and the Seven Dwarfs," " Rumplestiltskin," and "Tom Thumb." In each tale, the protagonist survives prejudice, imprisonment, ridicule, and even death to receive justice in a cruel world.

Older readers encounter a kind of fairy tale world in Shakespeare's *The Tempest* and *A Midsummer Night's Dream*, which use pixies and fairies as characters. Adolescent readers today are as fascinated by the creations of fantasy realms in the works of Piers Anthony, Ursula LeGuin, and Anne McCaffrey. An extension of interest in the supernatural is the popularity of science fiction that allows us to use current knowledge to predict the possible course of the future.

Angels (or sometimes fairy godmothers) play a role in some fairy tales, and Milton in Paradise Lost and Paradise Regained also used symbolic angels and devils.

Biblical stories provide many allusions. Parables, moralistic like fables but having human characters, include the stories of the Good Samaritan and the Prodigal Son. References to the treachery of Cain and the betrayal of Christ by Judas Iscariot are oft-cited examples.

American folk tales

American folktales are divided into two categories.

Imaginary tales, also called tall tales (humorous tales based on non-existent, fictional characters developed through blatant exaggeration)

> John Henry is a two-fisted steel driver who beats out a steam drill in competition.
>
> Rip Van Winkle sleeps for twenty years in the Catskill Mountains and upon awakening cannot understand why no one recognizes him.
>
> Paul Bunyan, a giant lumberjack, owns a great blue ox named Babe and has extraordinary physical strength. He is said to have plowed the Mississippi River while the impression of Babe's hoof prints created the Great Lakes.

Real tales, also called legends (based on real persons who accomplished the feats that are attributed to them even if they are slightly exaggerated)

For mre than forty years, Johnny Appleseed (John Chapman) roamed Ohio and Indiana planting apple seeds.

Daniel Boone - scout, adventurer, and pioneer - blazed the Wilderness Trail and made Kentucky safe for settlers.

Paul Revere, an colonial patriot, rode through the New England countryside warning of the approach of British troops.

George Washington cut down a cherry tree, which he could not deny, or did he?

SKILL 4.9 Apply various critical responses to literature.

Reading literature involves a reciprocal interaction between the reader and the text.

Types of responses

Emotional

The reader can identify with the characters and situations so as to project himself into the story. The reader feels a sense of satisfaction by associating aspects of his own life with the people, places, and events in the literature. Emotional responses are observed in a reader's verbal and non-verbal reactions - laughter, comments on its effects, and retelling or dramatizing the action.

Interpretive

Interpretive responses result in inferences about character development, setting, or plot; analysis of style elements - metaphor, simile, allusion, rhythm, tone; outcomes derivable from information provided in the narrative; and assessment of the author's intent. Interpretive responses are made verbally or in writing.

Critical

Critical responses involve making value judgments about the quality of a piece of literature. Reactions to the effectiveness of the writer's style and language use are observed through discussion and written reactions.

Evaluative

Some reading response theory researchers also add a response that considers the readers considerations of such factors as how well the piece of literature represents its genre, how well it reflects the social/ ethical mores of society, and how well the author has approached the subject for freshness and slant.

Middle school readers will exhibit both emotional and interpretive responses. Naturally, making interpretive responses depends on the degree of knowledge the student has of literary elements. A child's being able to say why a particular book was boring or why a particular poem made him sad evidences critical reactions on a fundamental level. Adolescents in ninth and tenth grades should begin to make critical responses by addressing the specific language and genre characteristics of literature. Evaluative responses are harder to detect and are rarely made by any but a few advanced high school students. However, if the teacher knows what to listen for, she can recognize evaluative responses and incorporate them into discussions.

For example, if a student says, "I don't understand why that character is doing that," he is making an interpretive response to character motivation. However, if he goes on to say, "What good is that action?" he is giving an evaluative response that should be explored in terms of "What good should it do and why isn't that positive action happening?"

At the emotional level, the student says, "I almost broke into a sweat when he was describing the heat in the burning house." An interpretive response says, "The author used descriptive adjectives to bring his setting to life." Critically, the student adds, "The author's use of descriptive language contributes to the success of the narrative and maintains reader interest through the whole story." If he goes on to wonder why the author allowed the grandmother in the story to die in the fire, he is making an evaluative response.

Levels of response

The levels of reader response will depend largely on the reader's level of social, psychological, and intellectual development. Most middle school students have progressed beyond merely involving themselves in the story enough to be able to retell the events in some logical sequence or describe the feeling that the story evoked. They are aware to some degree that the feeling evoked was the result of a careful manipulation of good elements of fiction writing. They may not explain that awareness as successfully as a high school student, but they are beginning to grasp the concepts and not just the personal reactions. They are beginning to differentiate between responding to the story itself and responding a literary creation.

Fostering self-esteem and empathy for others and the world in which one lives

All-important is the use of literature as bibliotherapy that allows the reader to identify with others and become aware of alternatives, yet not feeling directly betrayed or threatened. For the high school student the ability to empathize is an evaluative response, a much desired outcome of literature studies. Use of these books either individually or as a thematic unit of study allows for discussion or writing. The titles are grouped by theme, not by reading level.

ABUSE:

Blair, Maury and Brendel, Doug. *Maury, Wednesday's Child*

Dizenzo, Patricia. *Why Me?*

Parrot, Andrea. *Coping with Date Rape and Acquaintance Rape*

NATURAL WORLD CONCERNS:

Caduto, M. and Bruchac, J. *Keeper's of Earth*

Gay, Kathlyn. *Greenhouse Effect*

Johnson, Daenis. *Fiskadaro*

Madison, Arnold. *It Can't Happen to Me*

EATING DISORDERS:

Arnold, Caroline. *Too Fat, Too Thin, Do I Have a Choice?*

DeClements, Barthe. *Nothing's Fair in Fifth Grade*

Snyder, Anne. *Goodbye, Paper Doll*

FAMILY

Chopin, Kate. *The Runner*

Cormier, Robert. *Tunes for Bears to Dance to*

Danzinger, Paula. *The Divorce Express*

Neufield, John. *Sunday Father*

Okimoto, Jean Davies. *Molly by any Other Name*

Peck, Richard. *Don't Look and It Won't Hurt*

Zindel, Paul. *I Never Loved Your Mind*

STEREOTYPING:

Baklanov, Grigory. (Trans. by Antonina W. Bouis) *Forever Nineteen*

Kerr, M.E. *Gentle Lands*

Greene, Betty. *Summer of My German Soldier*

Reiss, Johanna. *The Upstairs Room*

Taylor, Mildred D. *Roll of Thunder, Hear Me Cry*

Wakatsuki-Houston, Jeanne and Houston, James D. *Farewell to Manzanar*

SUICIDE AND DEATH:

Blume, Judy. *Tiger Eyes*

Bunting, Eve. *If I Asked You, Would You Stay?*

Gunther, John. *Death Be Not Proud*

Mazer, Harry. *When the Phone Rings*

Peck, Richard. *Remembering the Good Times*

Richter, Elizabeth. *Losing Someone You Love*

Strasser, Todd. *Friends Till the End*

Cautions

There is always a caution when reading materials of a sensitive or controversial nature. The teacher must be cognizant of the happenings in the school and outside community to spare students undue suffering. A child who has known a recent death in his family or circle of friends may need to distance himself from classroom discussion. Whenever open discussion of a topic brings pain or embarrassment, the child should not be further subjected. Older children and young adults will be able to discuss issues with greater objectivity and without making blurted, insensitive comments. The teacher must be able to gauge the level of emotional development of her students when selecting subject matter and the strategies for studying it. The student or his parents may consider some material objectionable. Should a student choose not to read an assigned material, it is the teacher's responsibility to allow the student to select an alternate title. It is always advisable to notify parents if a particularly sensitive piece is to be studied.

SKILL 4.10 Demonstrate knowledge of resources for literature criticism.

Teachers should be familiar with professional resources that aid them in recognizing reader responses and teaching students the process of assessing their responses. One exceptional tool is Laurence Perrine's *Sound and Sense*, cited in the bibliography. Both the text itself and the teacher manual that accompanies it provide excellent examples of activities that contribute to the student's ability to make interpretive and evaluative responses.

There are also a variety of good student resources available in most school and public libraries that provide models of critical analyses. The Twayne publications are book length critiques of individual titles or of the body of work of a given author. The Modern Critical Interpretations series, edited by Harold Bloom, offers a collection of critical essays on individual titles in each book. Gale Research Company also provides several series: Nineteenth Century Literature Criticism, Twentieth Century Literature Criticism, and Contemporary Literary Criticism, to name a few. These encyclopedic sets contain reprints of literary magazine articles that date from the author's own lifetime to the present. Students doing independent research will find these are invaluable tools.

SKILL 4.11 Identify and demonstrate a variety of methods for teaching literature.

Studying literature requires more involvement of the student than traditional discussion/lecture processes have allowed. Literature, whether fiction, non-fiction, poetry, or drama, should not be studied for comprehension alone nor should detailed analyses of the elements of literature be an end in themselves. Literature is to be experienced if it is to be appreciated.

Teaching strategies

Reading/discussion

Reading, whether aloud or silently, evokes responses that can be verbalized. For young or below grade level readers, some sight-reading may be necessary. This should be done in small groups of two or three without teacher intervention. Students should feel free to discuss the text as they read. Most high school students should be able to participate in small group discussions of literature that has been read outside of class. During silent or at-home reading, the students should take notes of key elements as they read to enable them to contribute to subsequent discussions. Teacher guided discussion should transpire only after students have had a chance to think through the elements of the literature which are under study. Teacher led discussions should evolve from student responses to the reading not from preconceived interpretations by the teacher or recognized critics. Perceptive assessment of student comments will lead to questioning that probes the student's personal reactions and can ultimately be as analytical as any discussion the teacher might have planned.

Rather than involving the whole class, which favors the loquacious and inhibits the shy, let the students form into four or five discussion groups. After the initial discussion, have two groups join to share their reactions.

Dramatization

Young students need little encouragement to verbally retell stories to their classmates and to pantomime action. Older students should be given an opportunity to act out scenes not only from plays but also from other literature as well but only after planning and rehearsal. Treat the performance as a reflection of their appreciation for the work and not as a graded assignment. Middle school students become inhibited by solo performances so allow them to structure group performances. It is also important for students to view and listen to others performing and to show their appreciation for the performers as well as the literature.

Student writing

Encourage students to react honestly to literature. Allow them to choose their reading selections; if the choice is their own, their reactions can be more spontaneous and comfortable. With middle school/junior high students, keeping a reading diary may be as much as they can handle. High school students can be encouraged to write analytical reviews but try to keep them informal. Encourage students to read book reviews in current periodicals to see how critics express their responses.

Encourage students to attempt to write in certain genres. Have middle school students compose their own myths. High school students can try their hands at poems, short stories, and one-act plays. By attempting to write in a particular form, the student will gain a greater appreciation of the author's task.

Remember that teaching for appreciation and the encouragement of life-long reading means that instruction must be student centered. If you ever sat through a lecture in a college literature survey class, you can identify with the problems students have with lecturing in secondary schools. Teach the elements of literature and the process of learning through lecture, but avoid lecturing on the meaning of the literature at all costs. If you really want to inspire your students, perform the Lady Macbeth soliloquy or give your own book review - gratis. Read and write when they do and share your creativity with them. High school students are especially appreciative of a teacher who would never ask them to do something he cannot or will not do himself.

COMPETENCY 5.0 Demonstrate the ability to write competently on a topic.

SKILL 5.1 Write an essay reflecting literary skill.

GENERAL STRATEGIES FOR WRITING THE ESSAY

- Budget your time. You will not have time to revise your essay. It is important that you write a good first draft.

- Read the question carefully. Make sure you understand what the question is asking you to do.

- Review basic literary terms.

- Take time to prewrite.

- Write a thesis statement by restating the question.

- Keep your purpose in mind as you write your essay.

- Connect the ideas of your essay in a brief conclusion.

- Leave enough time to quickly proofread and edit your essay.

The essay that you are to write must demonstrate the ability to write on a literary topic. As you practice the steps provided to prepare for this test, please keep in mind that this review will not teach you how to analyze literature. It is expected that analyzing literature has been a focus of your course of study. The following steps in writing an essay in a timed situation will aid you in preparing to write the essay in the most time efficient manner possible. It is important to keep in mind that a good essay has focus, organization, support and correct usage.

Part I - Understanding the question

When you receive your question, the first thing you need to do is decide what the question is asking you to do. Look for key words that will establish the purpose of your essay. Examine the chart on the next page and review the key words and purpose each word establishes.

PRACTICE - Examine the chart on the following page. The chart identifies some of the key words you might find on an essay test. Please note that for each key word the purpose and an example are illustrated.

KEY WORD	PURPOSE	EXAMPLE
Analyze	To examine the parts of a literary selection	Read a passage and analyze how the author achieves tone using diction and imagery
Compare	To identify the similarities	Read "I Hear America Singing" by Walt Whitman and "Chicago" by Carl Sandburg and compare the similarities in each poet's attitude about America.
Contrast	To identify differences	Read "Thanatopsis" by Bryant and "Do Not Go Gentle Into That Good Night" by Dylan Thomas and contrast how each poet uses imagery to express his distinct views of death.
Discuss	Examine in detail	Read a poem and discuss how the poet establishes the mood using imagery and word choice.
Explain	Provide reasons, examples or clarify the meaning	Read the opening passage of *The Great Gatsby* and explain how the author establishes the tone of the novel.

When writing an essay on literature, consider the following things before you begin to prewrite.

** Identifying the elements for analysis. If you are asked to examine the tone of poem, you might need to look at imagery and word choice or if you are asked to examine prose and explain how a writer creates mood, it might be necessary to examine the diction, style, imagery, syntax, structure, and selection of detail.

** Deciding on your main idea. Use the question as a guideline. However, do not merely restate the question. Make sure that in restating the topic you have taken a position on how you will answer the prompt. For example, you might be asked to read Whitman's poem "I Hear America Singing" and discuss not only the tone of the poem, but also how Whitman creates the tone. It is important, if you wish to receive a high score on the essay, that your main idea clearly states what you think is the tone and how it is created.

** **Considering Audience, Purpose, and Tone**. Keep in mind that as you write this essay, your purpose is to demonstrate literary skill by reading an unfamiliar passage or poem and examining its elements. It is crucial to avoid giving a summary of the piece or writing your personal reaction to the work. Your audience is familiar with the piece and thus does not need to have the work summarized. In fact, the readers of your essay have been trained to look for focus, organization, support and correct usage. Finally, the tone is formal.

Part 2 - Prewriting for ideas and planning your essay

Prior to writing, you will need to prewrite for ideas and details as well as decide how the essay will be organized. In the hour you have to write you should spend no more than 5-10 minutes prewriting and organizing your ideas. As you prewrite, it might be helpful to remember you should have at least three main points and at least two to three details to support your main ideas. There are several types of graphic organizers that you should practice using as you prepare for the essay portion of the test.

PRACTICE - Choose one topic from the chart on page and complete the cluster.

PREWRITE TO EXPLAIN HOW OR WHY

Reread a question from the chart on the previous page that asks you to explain how a poet creates tone and mood use imagery and word choice. Then fill out the organizer on the following page that identifies how the poet effectively creates tone and mood. Support with examples from the poem.

VISUAL ORGANIZER: GIVING REASONS

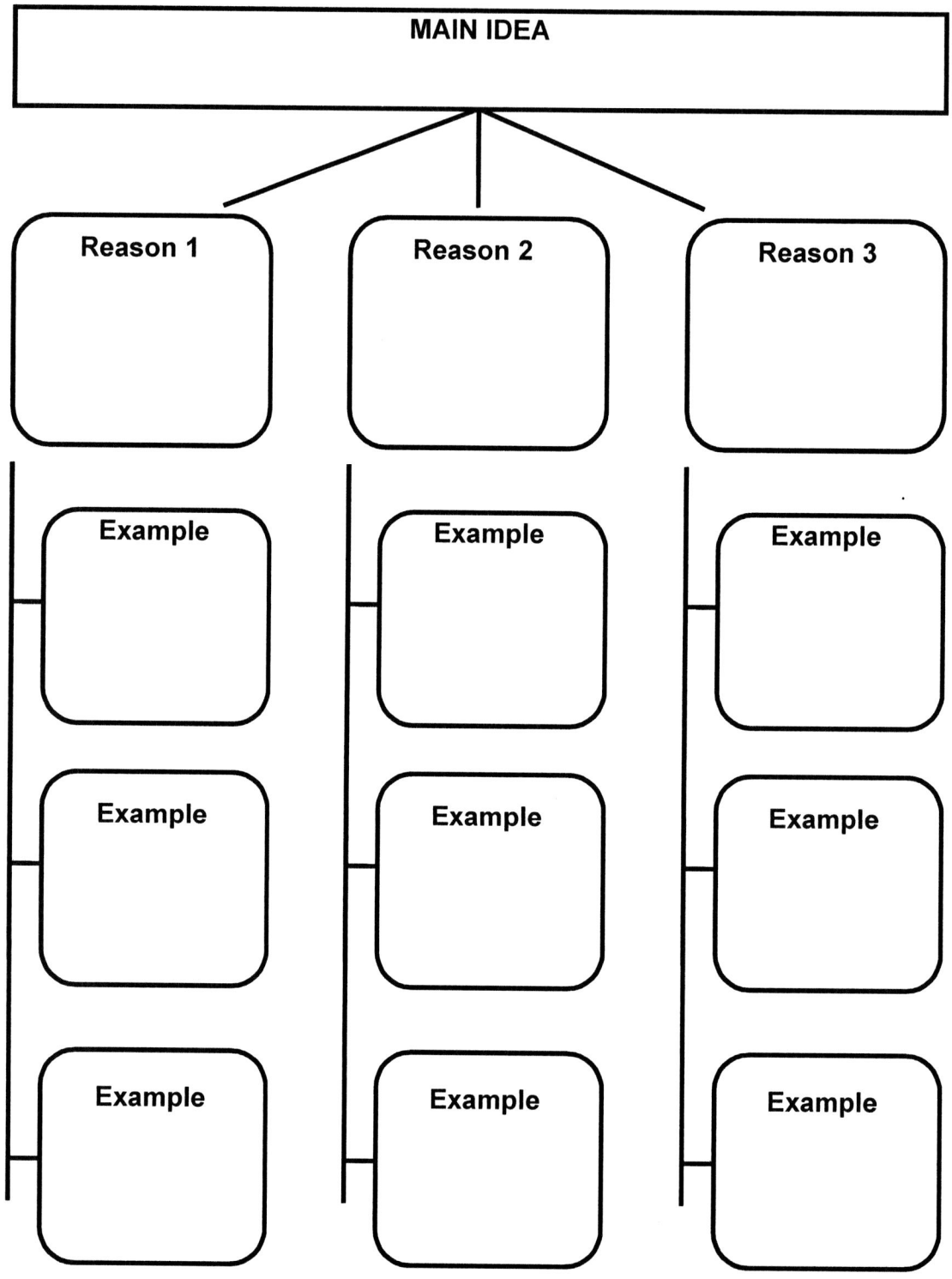

STEP 3: PREWRITE TO ORGANIZE IDEAS

After you have completed a graphic organizer, you need to decide how you will organize your essay. To organize your essay, you might consider one of the following patterns to structure your essay.

1. Examine individual elements such as **plot**, **setting**, **theme**, **character**, **point of view**, **tone**, **mood**, or **style**.

    SINGLE ELEMENT OUTLINE
    Intro - main idea statement
    Main point 1 with at least two supporting details
    Main point 2 with at least two supporting details
    Main point 3 with at least two supporting details
    Conclusion (restates main ideas and summary of main pts)

2. **Compare and contrast two elements**.

POINT-BY-POINT	BLOCK
Introduction Statement of main idea about A and B	Introduction Statement of main idea about A and B
Main Point 1 Discussion of A Discussion of B	Discussion of A Main Point 1 Main Point 2 Main point 3
Main Point 2 Discussion of A Discussion of B	Discussion of B Main Point 1 Main Point 2 Main Point 3
Main Point 3 Discussion of A Discussion of B	Conclusion Restate main idea
Conclusion Restatement or summary of main idea	

PRACTICE:
Using the cluster on the next page, choose an organizing chart and complete for your topic.

TEACHER CERTIFICATION EXAM

VISUAL ORGANIZER: GIVING INFORMATION

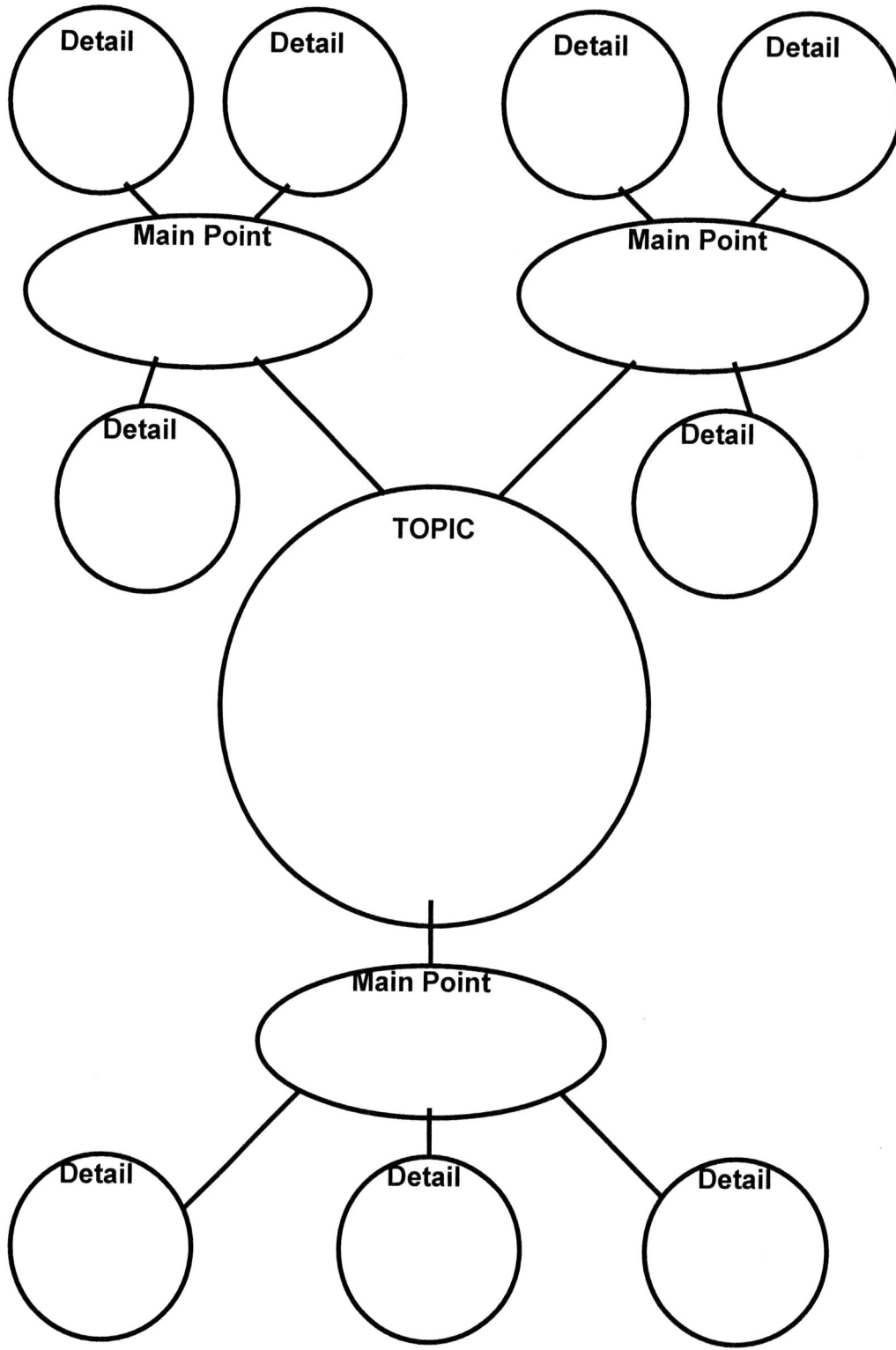

ENGLISH HIGH SCHOOL 112

Part 4 - Write The Thesis Statement

First: **Identify the topic.**

I am going to write about the tone and how it is created in the poem "I Hear America Singing" by Walt Whitman.

Second: **State your point of view about the topic.**

The upbeat and optimistic tone of Whitman's poem is created by his word choice, structure and imagery.

Third: **Summarize the main points you will make in your essay.**

Whitman creates an optimistic tone through his choice of words, parallel structure and images.

PRACTICE:
Using the topic and prewriting you completed on the previous page, write the Thesis Statement for your essay. Follow the steps outlined above.

ENGLISH HIGH SCHOOL

Part 5: State the main point of each body paragraph and organize support.

PARAGRAPH	PURPOSE	SUPPORT
1-INTRO	MAIN IDEA STATEMENT	
2-1ST BODY PARAGRAPH	MAIN POINT 1	QUOTES OR SPECIFICS FROM THE TEXT WITH ANALYSIS OR EXPLANATION OF HOW EACH DETAIL SUPPORTS YOUR MAIN POINT.
3-2ND BODY PARAGRAPH	MAIN POINT 2	QUOTES OR SPECIFICS FROM THE TEXT WITH ANALYSIS OR EXPLANATION OF HOW EACH DETAIL SUPPORTS YOUR MAIN POINT.
4-3RD BODY PARAGRAPH	MAIN POINT 3	QUOTES OR SPECIFICS FROM THE TEXT WITH ANALYSIS OR EXPLANATION OF HOW EACH DETAIL SUPPORTS YOUR MAIN POINT.
5-CLOSING	SUMMARIZE IDEAS	

PRACTICE:

Using the giving information cluster, complete your own organizing chart like the one above.

Part 6 - Write the introduction of your essay.

Remember that your introduction should accomplish the following things:

1. It should introduce the topic.

2. It should capture your reader's interest.

3. It should state your thesis.

4. It should prepare the reader for the main points of your essay.

TEACHER CERTIFICATION EXAM

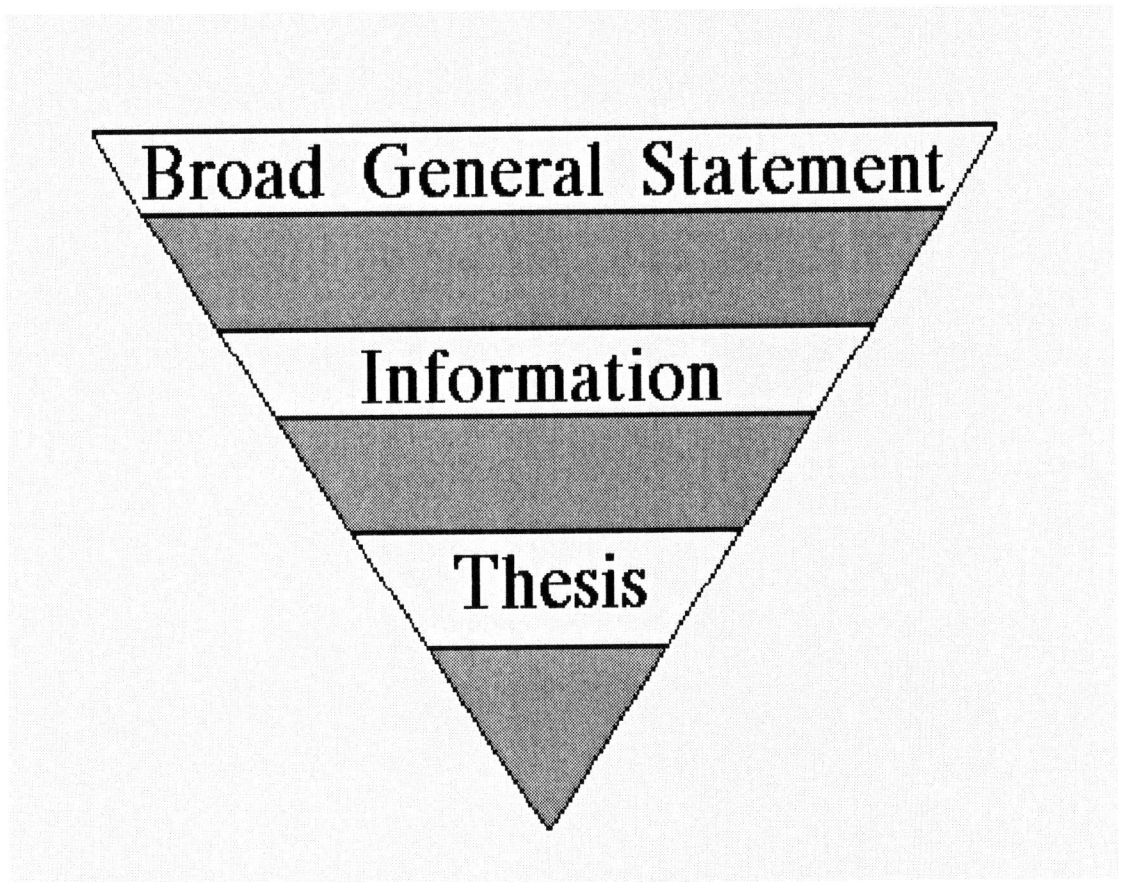

INVERTED TRIANGLE INTRODUCTION

Try to imagine the introduction as an inverted triangle. To write the introduction, follow the steps below.

1. On your prewriting sheet, write down your thesis. Check to see that you have made it specific, prepares the reader for what will follow, and clearly addresses the topic.

2. Open your introduction with a broad general statement.

3. Follow the broad general statement with one or more sentences that add interest and information about the topic.

4. Write your thesis at the end of the introduction.

PRACTICE:

Now, you are ready to write your introduction. Complete the steps for writing an introduction using the ideas from your prewriting and organizing chart.

Part 7 - Writing the body paragraphs

Once you have written your introduction, move on to the body paragraphs. Remember the follow guidelines as you write your body paragraphs.

Suggestions for Writing Body Paragraphs

* Write at least **three** body paragraphs.
* For each paragraph, you should write a main idea sentence, supporting details, and a closing sentence.
* Use transitions between and within each paragraph.
* Vary your sentence structure by using participial phrases, gerunds, infinitives and adjective and noun clauses.

PRACTICE:

Using your prewriting cluster and organizing chart, write the body paragraphs for your essay. Try to follow the suggestions listed above when writing your paragraphs.

Part 8 - Writing the conclusion

The closing paragraph of an essay summarizes the essay and reinforces the principal ideas of the essay. A good conclusion usually restates the thesis and main ideas from each body paragraph. It often ends with a clincher sentence, an unforgettable sentence that ends the paper.

PRACTICE:

Now, take out the essay for which you have already written an introduction and the body paragraphs. Write a conclusion to your essay and be sure to include a clincher sentence.

Part 9 - Editing and proofreading

On the Teacher Certification Examination - English middle school, you are being assessed on your ability to write an essay that demonstrates literary skill in a limited amount of time. You have sixty minutes to write; you will not have time to revise. However, correct usage will be a factor in your score. It is important to leave five minutes to reread, edit, and proofread your paper. In other testing situations, like the NTE, you may be given only a half hour to complete an essay that demands even greater organizational skills and less time for editing.

Editing occurs when you change words or phrases to clarify your ideas. If you make any changes, cross out the word or words once and write the new word or phrase directly above it. Make sure that any changes you make are clear.

Proofreading is checking your essay for any errors in mechanics or punctuation. Although you are writing in a timed situation, you are expected to follow the standards of correct usage. If you find an error, cross it out with a single line and write the correction directly above the error.

PRACTICE:

Take out the essay for which you have written an introduction, a body, and a conclusion. Take five minutes to edit and proofread your essay.

FINAL PREPARATIONS

Practice the steps outlined here on one of the following topics or you can use questions posed in some of your own English classes. Keep in mind that often the essay question on the exam asks you to read an unfamiliar passage or poem and write an essay that expresses a point of view, uses logical reasoning, and supports ideas with specifics.

TEACHER CERTIFICATION EXAM

RESOURCES

1. Abrams, M. H. ed. *The Norton Anthology of English Literature.* 6th ed. 2 vols. New York: Norton, 1979.

   A comprehensive reference for English literature, containing selected works from *Beowulf* through the twentieth century and information about literary criticism.

2. Beach, Richard. "Strategic Teaching in Literature." *Strategic Teaching and Learning: Cognitive Instruction in the Content Areas.* Edited by Beau Fly Jones and others. ASCD Publications, 1987: 135-159.

   A chapter dealing with a definition of and strategic teaching strategies for literature studies.

3. Brown, A. C. and others. *Grammar and Composition 3rd Course.* Boston: Houghton Mifflin, 1984.

   A standard ninth-grade grammar text covering spelling, vocabulary, and reading, listening, and writing skills.

4. Burmeister, L. E. *Reading Strategies for Middle and Secondary School Teachers.* Reading, MA: Addison-Wesley, 1978.

   A resource for developing classrooms strategies for reading and content area classes, using library references, and adapting reading materials to all levels of students.

5. Carrier, W. and B. Neumann, eds. *Literature from the World.* New York: Scribner, 1981.

   A comprehensive world literature text for high school students, with a section on mythology and folklore.

6. Cline, R. K. J. and W. G. McBride. *A Guide to Literature for Young Adults: Background, Selection, and Use.* Glenview, IL: Scott Foresman, 1983.

   A literature reference containing sample readings and an overview of adolescent literature and the developmental changes that affect reading.

7. Coater, Jr. R. B., ed. *Reading Research and Instruction.* Journal of the College Research Association. Pittsburgh, PA : 1995.

   A reference tool for reading and language arts teachers, covering the latest research and instructional techniques.

8. Corcoran, B. and E. Evans, eds. *Readers, Texts, Teachers.* Upper Montclair, NJ: Boynton/Cook, 1987.

   A collection of essays concerning reader response theory, including activities that help students interpret literature and help the teacher integrate literature into the course study.

9. Cutting, Brian. *Moving on in Whole Language: the Complete Guide for Every Teacher.* Bothell, WA: Wright Group, 1992.

   A resource of practical knowledge in whole language instruction.

10. Damrosch, L. and others. *Adventures in English Literature.* Orlando, FL: Harcourt, Brace, Jovanovich, 1985.

    One of many standard high school English literature textbooks with a solid section on the development of the English language.

11. Davidson, A. *Literacy 2000 Teacher's Resource. Emergent Stages 1&2.* 1990.

12. Devine, T. G. *Teaching Study Skills: A Guide for Teachers.* Boston: Allyn and Bacon, 1981.

13. Duffy, G. G. and others. *Comprehension Instruction: Perspectives and Suggestions.* New York: Longman, 1984.

    Written by researchers at the Institute of Research on Teaching and the Center for the Study of Reading, this reference includes a variety of instructional techniques for different levels.

14. Fleming, M. ed. *Teaching the Epic.* Urbana, IL: NCTE, 1974.

    Methods, materials, and projects for the teaching of epics with examples of Greek, religious, national, and American epics.

15. Flood, J. ed. *Understanding Reading Comprehension: Cognition, Language, and the Structure of Prose.* Newark, DE: IRA, 1984.

    Essays by preeminent scholars dealing with comprehension for learners of all levels and abilities.

16. Fry, E. B. and others. *The Reading Teacher's Book of Lists.* Edgewood Cliffs, NJ: Prentice-Hall, 1984.

    A comprehensive list of book lists for students of various reading levels.

17. Garnica, Olga K. and Martha L. King. *Language, Children, and Society.* New York: Pergamon Press, 1981.

18. Gere, A. R. and E. Smith. *Attitude, Language and Change.* Urbana, IL: NCTE, 1979.

    A discussion of the relationship between standard English and grammar and the vernacular usage, including various approaches to language instruction.

19. Hayakawa, S. I. *Language in Thought and Action.* 4th ed. Orlando, Fl: Harcourt, Brace, Jovanovich, 1979.

20. Hook, J. N. and others. *What Every English Teacher Should Know.* Champaign, IL: NCTE, 1970.

    Research based text that summarizes methodologies and specific application for us with students.

21. Johnson, D. D. and P. D. Pearson. *Teaching Reading Vocabulary.* 2nd ed. New York: Holt, Rinehart, and Winston, 1984.

    A student text that stresses using vocabulary study in improving reading comprehension, with chapters on instruction components in the reading and content areas.

22. Kaywell, I. F. ed. *Adolescent Literature as a Complement to the Classics.* Norwood, MA: Christopher-Gordon Pub., 1993.

    A correlation of modern adolescent literature to classics of similar themes.

23. Mack, M. ed. *World Masterpieces*. 3rd ed. 2 vols. New York: Norton, 1973.

    A standard world literature survey, with good introductory material on a critical approach to literature study.

24. McLuhan, M. *Understanding Media: The Extensions of Man.* New York: Signet, 1964.

    The most classic work on the effect media has on the public and the power of the media to influence thinking.

25. McMichael, G. ed. *Concise Anthology of American Literature.* New York: Macmillan, 1974.

    A standard survey of American literature text.

26. Moffett, J. *Teaching the Universe of Discourse.* Boston: Houghton Mifflin, 1983.

    A significant reference text that proposes the outline for a total language arts program, emphasizing the reinforcement of each element of the language arts curriculum to the other elements.

27. Moffett, James and Betty Jane Wagner. *Student - Centered Language Arts K-12*. 4th ed. Boston: Houghton Mifflin, 1992.

28. Nelms, B. F. ed. *Literature in the Classroom: Readers, Texts, and Contexts.* Urbana, IL: NCTE, 1988.

    Essays on adolescent and multicultural literature, social aspects of literature, and approaches to literature interpretation.

29. Nilsen, A. P. and K. L. Donelson. *Literature for Today's Young Adults.* 2nd ed. Glenview, IL: Scott, Foresman, and Co., 1985.

    An excellent overview of young adult literature - its history, terminologies, bibliographies, and book reviews.

30. Perrine, L. *Literature: Structure, Sound, and Sense.* 5th ed. Orlando, FL: Harcourt, Brace, Jovanovich, 1988.

    A much revised text for teaching literature elements, genres, and interpretation.

31. Piercey, Dorothy. *Reading Activities in Content Areas: An Ideabook for Middle and Secondary Schools.* 2nd ed. Boston: Allyn and Bacon, 1982.

32. Pooley, R. C. *The Teaching of English Usage.* Urbana, IL: NCTE, 1974.

   A revision of the important 1946 text which discusses the attitudes toward English usage through history and recommends specific techniques for usage instruction.

33. Probst, R. E. *Response and Analysis: Teaching Literature in Junior and Senior High School.* Upper Montclair, NJ: Boynton/Cook, 1988.

   A resource that explores reader response theory and discusses student-centered methods for interpreting literature. Contains a section on the progress of adolescent literature.

34. Pyles, T. and J. Alges. *The Origin and Development of the English Language.* 3rd ed. Orlando, FL: Harcourt, Brace, Jovanovich, 1982.

   A history of the English language; sections social, personal, historical, and geographical influences on language usage.

35. Readence, J. E. and others. *Content Area Reading: an integrated approach.* 2nd ed. Dubuque, IA: Kendall/Hunt, 1985.

   A practical instruction guide for teaching reading in the content areas.

36. Robinson, H. Alan. *Teaching Reading and Study Strategies: The Content Areas.* Boston: Allyn and Bacon, 1978.

37. Roe, B. D. and others. *Secondary School Reading Instruction: The Content Areas.* 3rd ed. Boston: Houghton Mifflin, 1987.

   A resource of strategies for the teaching of reading for language arts teachers with little reading instruction background.

38. Rosenberg, D. *World Mythology: An Anthology of the Great Myths and Epics.* Lincolnwood, IL: National Textbook, 1986.

   Presents selections of main myths from which literary allusions are drawn. Thorough literary analysis of each selection.

39. Rosenblatt, L. M. *The Reader, the Text, the Poem. The Transactional Theory of the Literary work.* Southern Illinois University Press, 1978.

   A discussion of reader response theory and reader-centered methods for analyzing literature.

40. Santeusanio, Richard P. *A Practical Approach to Content Area Reading.* Reading, MA.: Addison-Wesley Publishing Co., 1983.

41. Shepherd, David L. *Comprehensive High School Reading Methods.* 2nd ed. Columbus, OH: Charles F. Merrill Publishing, 1978.

42. Strickland, D. S. and others. *Using Computers in the Teaching of Reading.* New York: Teachers College Press, 1987.

   Resource for strategies for teaching and learning language and reading with computers and recommendations for software for all grades.

43. Sutherland, Zena and others. *Children and Books.* 6th ed. Glenview, IL: Scott, Foresman, and Co., 1981.

   Thorough study of children's literature, with sections on language development theory and chapters on specific genres with synopses of specific classic works for child/adolescent readers.

44. Tchudi, S. and D. Mitchell. *Explorations in the Teaching of English.* 3rd ed. New York: Harper Row, 1989.

   A thorough source of strategies for creating a more student-centered involvement in learning.

45. Tompkins, Gail E. *Teaching Writing: Balancing Process and Product.* 2nd ed. New York: Macmillan, 1994.

   A tool to aid teachers in integrating recent research and theory about the writing process, writing reading connections, collaborative learning, and across the curriculum writing with practices in the fourth through eighth grade classrooms.

46. Warriners, J. E. *English Composition and Grammar.* Benchmark ed. Orlando, FL: Harcourt, Brace, Jovanovich, 1988.

   Standard grammar and composition textbook, with a six book series for seventh through twelfth grades; includes vocabulary study, language history, and diverse approaches to writing process.

THIS PAGE INTENTIONALLY LEFT BLANK.

TEACHER CERTIFICATION EXAM

Section I: **Essay Test**

Given are several prompts, reflecting the need to exhibit a variety of writing skills. In most testing situations, 30 minutes would be allowed to respond to each of the prompts. Some tests may allow 60 minutes for the essay to incorporate more than one question or allow for greater preparation and editing time. Read the directions carefully and organize your time wisely.

Section II: **Multiple - choice Test**

This section contains 125 questions. In most testing situations, you would be expected to answer from 35 - 40 questions within 30 minutes. If you time yourself on the entire battery, take no more than 90 minutes.

Section III: **Answer Key**

TEACHER CERTIFICATION EXAM

Section I: Essay Prompts

Prompt A

Write an expository essay discussing effective teaching strategies for developing literature appreciation with a heterogeneous class of ninth graders. Select any appropriate piece(s) of world literature to use as examples in the discussion.

Prompt B

After reading the following passage from Aldous Huxley's *Brave New World,* discuss the types of reader responses possible with a group of college-bound seniors.

> "He hated them all - all the men who came to visit Linda. One afternoon, when he had been playing with the other children - it was cold, he remembered, and there was snow on the mountains - he came back to the house and heard angry voices in the bedroom. They were women's voices, and they were words he didn't understand; but he knew they were dreadful words. Then suddenly, crash! something was upset; he heard people moving about quickly, and there was another crash and then a noise like hitting a mule, only not so bony; then Linda screamed. 'Oh, don't, don't, don't!' she said. He ran in. There were three women in dark blankets. Linda was on the bed. One of the women was holding her wrists. Another was lying across her legs, so she couldn't kick. The third was hitting her with a whip. Once, twice, three times; and each time Linda screamed."

Prompt C

Write a persuasive letter to the editor on any contemporary topic of special interest. Employ whatever forms of discourse, style devices, and audience appeal techniques that seem appropriate to the topic.

ENGLISH HIGH SCHOOL

TEACHER CERTIFICATION EXAM

Section II: Writing and Language Skills

Part A

Directions: In sentences 1 - 15, four words or phrases have been underlined. If you determine that any underlined word or phrase has an error in grammar, usage, or mechanics, circle the letter underneath the underlining. If there are no errors, circle the letter E at the end of the sentence. There is no more than one error in any sentence.

1. The volcanic eruption in Montserrat displaced residents of Plymouth <u>which</u>
                                                                                                             A
   felt that the <u>English government</u> <u>was</u> responsible for <u>their</u> evacuation. **E**
                 B   **C**   **D**

2. When the <u>school district</u> privatized the school cafeteria, <u>us</u> students <u>were</u>
                 A   **B**   **C**
   thrilled to purchase more than soggy <u>French fries</u>. **E**
                                          D

3. The home coming <u>Queen and King</u> <u>were chosen</u> by the <u>student body</u> for
                      A   **B**   **C**
   <u>their</u> popularity. **E**
   D

4. If the practical joke <u>was</u> <u>Cullen's</u> idea, then he <u>must</u> suffer the
                       A **B**   **C**
   <u>consequences</u>. **E**
   D

5. She, not her sister, <u>is</u> the one <u>who</u> the librarian <u>has questioned</u> about the
                       A   **B**   **C**
   missing books, <u>Butterfly's</u> Ball and the Bears' House. **E**
                     D

6. Jack told a <u>credulous</u> story about his trip <u>up the beanstalk</u> because each
              A   **B**
   child in the room <u>was convinced</u> <u>by his reasoning</u>. **E**
                    C   **D**

7. There <u>are</u> <u>fewer</u> students in school this year despite the <u>principal's</u>
         A **B**   **C**
   prediction of <u>increasing</u> enrollment. **E**
               D

ENGLISH HIGH SCHOOL

TEACHER CERTIFICATION EXAM

8. My mother is a <u>Methodist</u>. She married a <u>Southern Baptist</u> and took <u>us</u>
                   A   B   C

   children to the <u>First Baptist church</u> in Stuart. E
                      D

9. When we moved from Jacksonvill<u>e,</u> to Little Roc<u>k,</u> Arkansas, my
                                          A   B

   <u>Dad</u> <u>was promoted</u> to store manager. E
    C   D

10. "One of the <u>burglar's</u> was <u>already</u> <u>apprehended</u> before his colleagues
                        A   B   C

    left the buildin<u>g,"</u> bragged the officer. E
              D

11. Walter said <u>that</u> his calculator <u>has been missing</u> <u>since</u> last Monday
                 A   B   C

    <u>responding to my question</u>. E
             D

12. Why was the girl <u>that</u> had plenty of money <u>arrested</u> for <u>shoplifting</u> some
                 A   B   C

    trinkets of <u>two dollar's worth</u>? E
             D

13. The future <u>will be</u> <u>because of</u> the past; <u>by changing the past</u> <u>would alter</u>
            A   B   C   D

    the future. E

14. <u>Mr. Thomas'</u> daughter-in-law encouraged her <u>husband's</u> boss to host a
        A   B

    fund-raiser for <u>the United Way</u>, a charity that Mr. Thomas <u>supports</u>. E
                     B   D

15. Miriam decided to remain <u>stationary</u> <u>since</u> <u>to move</u> would startle the horses,
                                   A   B   C

    one of <u>which</u> might bolt. E
            D

TEACHER CERTIFICATION EXAM

Part B

Directions: Each underlined portion of sentences 16 - 25 contains one or more errors in grammar, usage, mechanics, or sentence structure. Circle the choice which best corrects the error without changing the meaning of the original sentence. Choice D or E repeats the underlined portion. Select the identical phrase if you find no errors.

16. Joe **didn't hardly know his cousin Fred** who'd had a rhinoplasty.

   A. hardly did know his cousin Fred
   B. didn't know his cousin Fred hardly
   C. hardly knew his cousin Fred
   D. didn't know his cousin Fred
   E. didn't hardly know his cousin Fred

17. **Mixing the batter for cookies,** the cat licked the Crisco from the cookie sheet.

   A. While mixing the batter for cookies
   B. While the batter for cookies was mixing
   C. While I mixed the batter for cookies
   D. While I mixed the cookies
   E. Mixing the batter for cookies

18. Mr. Brown is a school volunteer **with a reputation and twenty years service.**

   A. with a reputation for twenty years' service
   B. with a reputation for twenty year's service
   C. who has served twenty years
   D. with a service reputation of twenty years
   E. with a reputation and twenty years service

ENGLISH HIGH SCHOOL

19. **Walt Whitman was famous for his composition, *Leaves of Grass*, serving as a nurse during the Civil War, and a devoted son.**

    A. *Leaves of Grass*, his service as a nurse during the Civil War, and a devoted son

    B. composing *Leaves of Grass*, serving as a nurse during the Civil War, and being a \ devoted son

    C. his composition, *Leaves of Grass*, his nursing during the Civil War, and his devotion as a son

    D. having authored *Leaves of Grass*, served as a nurse during the Civil War, and as a devoted son

    E. his composition, *Leaves of Grass*, serving as a nurse during the Civil War, and a devoted son.

20. **A teacher must know not only her subject matter but also the strategies of content teaching.**

    A. must not only know her subject matter but also the strategies of content teaching

    B. not only must know her subject matter but also the strategies of content teaching

    C. must not know only her subject matter but also the strategies of content teaching

    D. must know not only her subject matter but also the strategies of content teaching

21. **My English teacher, Mrs. Hunt, is nicer than any teacher at school and is the most helpful.**

    A. is as nice as any teacher at school and is

    B. is nicer than any other teacher at school and is

    C. is as nice as any other teacher at school and is

    D. is nicer than any teacher at school and is

TEACHER CERTIFICATION EXAM

22. **The teacher implied from our angry words that there was conflict between you and me.**

    A. implied ... between you and I

    B. inferred... between you and I

    C. inferred...between you and me

    D. implied ... between you and me

23. **There were fewer pieces of evidence presented during the second trial.**

    A. fewer peaces

    B. less peaces

    C. less pieces

    D. fewer pieces

24. **Mr. Smith respectfully submitted his resignation and had a new job.**

    A. respectively submitted his resignation and has

    B. respectively submitted his resignation before accepting

    C. respectfully submitted his resignation because of

    D. respectfully submitted his resignation and had

25. **Wally groaned, "Why do I have to do an oral interpretation of "The Raven."**

    A. groaned "Why ... of 'The Raven' ?"

    B. groaned "Why ... of "The Raven" ?

    C. groaned ",Why ... of "The Raven ?"

    D. groaned, "Why ... of "The Raven."

TEACHER CERTIFICATION EXAM

Part C

Directions: Select the best answer in each group of multiple choices.

26. The synonyms "gyro," "hero," and "submarine" reflect which influence on language usage?

    A. social

    B. geographical

    C. historical

    D. personal

27. The following passage is written from which point of view?

    As she mused the pitiful vision of her mother's life laid its spell on the very quick of her being - that life of commonplace sacrifices closing in final craziness. She trembled as she heard again her mother's voice saying constantly with foolish insistence: Derevaun Seraun! Derevaun Seraun !*
    * "The end of pleasure is pain!" (Gaelic)

    A. First person, narrator

    B. Second person, direct address

    C. Third person, omniscient

    D. First person, omniscient

28. The literary device of personification is used in which example below?

    A. "Beg me no beggary by soul or parents, whining dog!"

    B. "Happiness sped through the halls cajoling as it went."

    C. "O wind thy horn, thou proud fellow."

    D. "And that one talent which is death to hide."

29. Which of the writers below is a renowned Black poet?

    A. Maya Angelou

    B. Sandra Cisneros

    C. Richard Wilbur

    D. Richard Wright

30. Which of the following is not one of the four forms of discourse?

    A. exposition

    B. description

    C. rhetoric

    D. persuasion

ENGLISH HIGH SCHOOL

31. **Among junior-high school students of low-to-average readability levels which work would most likely stir reading interest?**

    A. *Elmer Gantry*, Sinclair Lewis

    B. *Smiley's People*, John LeCarre

    C. *The Outsiders*, S. E. Hinton

    D. *And Then There Were None*, Agatha Christie

32. **"Every one must pass through Vanity Fair to get to the celestial city" is an allusion from a**

    A. Chinese folk tale.

    B. Norse saga.

    C. British allegory.

    D. German fairy tale.

33. **Which teaching method would be most effective for interesting underachievers in the required senior English class?**

    A. Assign use of glossary work and extensively footnoted excerpts of great works.

    B. Have students take turns reading aloud the anthology selection.

    C. Let students choose which readings they'll study and write about.

    D. Use a chronologically arranged, traditional text, but assigning group work, panel presentations, and portfolio management.

34. **Which poem is typified as a villanelle?**

    A. "Do not Go Gentle into That Good Night"

    B. "Dover Beach"

    C. *Sir Gawain and the Green Knight*

    D. *Pilgrim's Progress*

35. Which term best describes the form of the following poetic excerpts?

And more to lulle him in his slumber soft,
A trickling streame from high rock tumbling downe,
And ever-drizzling raine upon the loft.
Mixt with a murmuring winde, much like a swowne
No other noyse, nor peoples troubles cryes.
As still we wont t'annoy the walle'd towne,
Might there be heard: but careless Quiet lyes,
Wrapt in eternall silence farre from enemyes.

A. Ballad

B. Elegy

C. Spenserian stanza

D. Octava rima

36. Which poet was a major figure in the Harlem Renaissance?

A. e. e. cummings

B. Rita Dove

C. Margaret Atwood

D. Langston Hughes

37. To understand the origins of a word, one must study the

A. synonyms.

B. inflections.

C. phonetics.

D. etymology.

38. Which sonnet form describes the following?

My galley charg'ed with forgetfulness
　Through sharp seas, in winter night doth pass
'Tween rock and rock; and eke mine enemy, alas,
That is my lord steereth with cruelness.
And every oar a thought in readiness,
　As though that death were light in such a case.
　An endless wind doth tear the sail apace
　Or forc'ed sighs and trusty fearfulness.
A rain of tears, a cloud of dark disdain,
　Hath done the wearied cords great hinderance,
Wreathed with error and eke with ignorance.
　The stars be hid that led me to this pain
　Drowned is reason that should me consort,
　And I remain despairing of the poet.

A. Petrarchan or Italian sonnet

B. Shakespearean or Elizabethan sonnet

C. Romantic sonnet

D. Spenserian sonnet

39. What is the salient literary feature of this excerpt from an epic?

Hither the heroes and the nymphs resort,
To taste awhile the pleasures of a court;
In various talk th'instructive hours they passed,
Who gave the ball, or paid the visit last;
One speaks the glory of the English Queen,
And another describes a charming Indian screen;
A third interprets motion, looks and eyes;
At every word a reputation dies.

A. Sprung rhythm

B. Onomatopoeia

C. Heroic couplets

D. Motif

40. What were two major characteristics of the first American literature?

A. Vengefulness and arrogance

B. Bellicosity and derision

C. Oral delivery and reverence for the land

D. Maudlin and self-pitying egocentricism

41. Arthur Miller wrote *The Crucible* as a parallel to what twentieth century event?

    A. Sen. McCarthy's House un-American Activities Committee Hearing

    B. The Cold War

    C. The fall of the Berlin Wall

    D. The Persian Gulf War

42. Latin words that entered the English language during the Elizabethan Age include

    A. allusion, education, and esteem.

    B. vogue and mustache.

    C. canoe and cannibal.

    D. alligator, cocoa, and armadillo.

43. Which of the following is not a characteristic of a fable?

    A. animals that feel and talk like humans.

    B. happy solutions to human dilemmas.

    C. teaches a moral or standard for behavior.

    D. illustrates specific people or groups without directly naming them.

44. An example of the subject of a tall-tale is

    A. John Henry.

    B. Paul Bunyan.

    C. George Washington.

    D. Rip Van Winkle.

45. If a student has a poor vocabulary the teacher should recommend that

    A. the student read newspapers, magazines and books on a regular basis.

    B. the student enroll in a Latin class.

    C. the student write the words repetitively after looking them up in the dictionary.

    D. the student use a thesaurus to locate synonyms and incorporate them into his/her vocabulary.

46. Which author did not write satire?

    A. Joseph Addison

    B. Richard Steele

    C. Alexander Pope

    D. John Bunyan

47. Which of the following was not written by Jonathan Swift?

    A. "A Voyage to Lilliput"

    B. "A Modest Proposal"

    C. "Samson Agonistes"

    D. "A Tale of a Tub"

48. Which is not a Biblical allusion?

    A. The patience of Job

    B. Thirty pieces of silver

    C. "Man proposes; God disposes"

    D. "Suffer not yourself to be betrayed by a kiss"

49. Which definition below is the best for defining diction?

    A. The specific word choices of an author to create a particular mood or feeling in the reader.

    B. Writing which explains something thoroughly.

    C. The background, or exposition, for a short story or drama.

    D. Word choices which help teach a truth or moral.

50. Which is the best definition of free verse, or *vers libre*?

    A. Poetry which consists of an unaccented syllable followed by an unaccented sound.

    B. Short lyrical poetry written to entertain but with an instructive purpose.

    C. Poetry which does not have a uniform pattern of rhythm.

    D. A poem which tells a story and has a plot.

51. Which is not an accepted point of view in literary works?

    A. First person, omniscient

    B. Third person, narrative

    C. First person, limited

    D. Third person, internal

52. **Which is an untrue statement about a theme in literature?**

    A. The theme is always stated directly somewhere in the text.

    B. The theme is the central idea in a literary work.

    C. All parts of the work (plot, setting, mood) should contribute to the theme in some way.

    D. By analyzing the various elements of the work, the reader should be able to arrive at an indirectly stated theme.

53. **Which is not a true statement concerning an author's literary tone?**

    A. Tone is partly revealed through the selection of details.

    B. Tone is the expression of the author's attitude toward his/her subject.

    C. Tone in literature is usually satiric or angry.

    D. Tone in literature corresponds to the tone of voice a speaker uses.

54. **In the teaching of poetry, the teacher should include all of the following but one. Select the answer which is not appropriate for all poetry instruction.**

    A. Setting and audience

    B. Theme and tone

    C. Pattern and diction

    D. Diction and rhyme scheme

55. **Which of the following definitions best describes a parable?**

    A. A short entertaining account of some happening, usually using talking animals as characters.

    B. A slow, sad song or poem, or prose work expressing lamentation.

    C. An extended narrative work expressing universal truths concerning domestic life.

    D. A short, simple story of an occurrence of a familiar kind, from which a moral or religious lesson may be drawn.

TEACHER CERTIFICATION EXAM

56. Which of the following is the best definition of existentialism?

A. The philosophical doctrine that matter is the only reality and that everything in the world, including thought, will and feeling, can be explained only in terms of matter.

B. Philosophy which views things as they should be or as one would wish them to be.

C. A philosophical and literary movement, variously religious and atheistic, stemming from Kierkegaard and represented by Sartre.

D. The belief that all events are determined by fate and are hence inevitable.

57. Which of the following is the best definition of imagism?

A. A doctrine which teaches that comfort is the only goal of value in life.

B. A movement in modern poetry (c 1910-1918) characterized by precise, concrete images, free verse, and suggestion rather than complete statement.

C. The belief that people are motivated in all their only by self-centeredness.

D. The doctrine that the human mind cannot know where there is a God or an ultimate cause, or anything beyond material phenomenon.

58. Which definition below best fits that of naturalism?

   A. Belief that the writer or artist should apply scientific objectivity in his/her observation and treatment of life without imposing value of judgments.

   B. The doctrine that teaches that the existing world is the best to be hoped for.

   C. The doctrine which teaches that God is not a personality, but that all laws, forces and manifestations of the universe are God-related.

   D. A philosophical doctrine which professes that the truth of all knowledge must always be in question.

59. The tendency to emphasize and value the qualities and peculiarities of life in a particular area of geographic site is a definition of

   A. pragmatism.

   B. regionalism.

   C. pantheism.

   D. abstractionism.

60. A traditional, anonymous story ostensibly with a historical basis, serving usually to explain some phenomenon of nature or the creation of earth and mankind, for example, is a definition of a

   A. proverb.

   B. idyll.

   C. myth.

   D. epic.

61. The arrangement and relationship of words in sentences or sentence structure best describes

   A. style.

   B. discourse.

   C. thesis.

   D. syntax.

62. A form of discourse which explains or informs is

   A. exposition

   B. narration.

   C. persuasion.

   D. description.

63. The substitution of "went to his rest" for "died" is an example of a/an

    A. bowdlerism.

    B. jargon.

    C. euphemism.

    D. malapropism

64. A conversation between two or more people is called a

    A. parody.

    B. dialogue.

    C. monologue.

    D. analogy.

65. "Clean as a whistle" or "Easy as falling of a log" are examples of

    A. semantics.

    B. parody.

    C. irony.

    D. clichés.

66. Which of the following is most true of expository writing?

    A. It is mutually exclusive of other forms of discourse.

    B. It can incorporate other forms of discourse in the process of providing supporting details.

    C. It should never employ informal expression.

    D. It should only be scored with an summative evaluation.

67. The appearance of a Yankee from Connecticut in the Court of King Arthur is an example of a/an

    A. rhetoric.

    B. parody.

    C. paradox.

    D. anachronism

68. The quality in a work of literature which evokes feelings of pity or compassion is called

    A. colloquy.

    B. irony.

    C. pathos.

    D. paradox.

69. "I'll die if I don't pass this course" is an example of

   A. barbarism.

   B. oxymoron.

   C. hyperbole.

   D. antithesis.

70. An extended metaphor which compares two very dissimilar things - one lofty, one lowly, is a definition of a/an

   A. antithesis.

   B. aphorism.

   C. apostrophe.

   D. conceit.

71. A figure of speech in which someone absent or something inhuman is addressed as though present and able to respond describes

   A. personification.

   B. synecdoche.

   C. metonymy.

   D. apostrophe.

72. Certain slang or jargon expressions peculiar to a certain ethnicity, age, economic, or professional group are called

   A. aphorisms.

   B. allusions.

   C. idioms.

   D. euphemisms.

73. Which of the following is a complex sentence?

   A. Anna and Margaret read a total of fifty-four books during summer vacation.

   B. The youngest boy on the team had the best earned run average which mystifies the coaching staff.

   C. Earl decided to attend Princeton; his twin brother Roy, who aced the ASVAB test, will be going to Annapolis.

   D. "Easy come, easy go," Marcia moaned.

74. Followers of Piaget's learning theory believe that adolescents in the formal operations period

   A. behave properly from fear of punishment rather than from a conscious decision to take a certain action.

   B. see the past more realistically and can relate to people from the past more than preadolescents.

   C. are less self-conscious and thus more willing to project their own identities into those of fictional characters.

   D. have not yet developed a symbolic imagination.

75. Which of the following is a formal reading level assessment?

   A. a standardized reading test

   B. a teacher-made reading test

   C. an interview

   D. a reading diary.

76. Middle and high school students are more receptive to studying grammar and syntax

   A. through worksheets and end of lesson practices in textbooks.

   B. through independent, homework assignments.

   C. through analytical examination of the writings of famous authors.

   D. though application to their own writing.

77. Which statement below best describes an author and his/her work?

   A. Zora Neale Hurston's *Their Eyes Were Watching God* dealt autobiographically with the strong faith that helped her through the years of her poor upbringing in rural Florida.

   B. Willa Cather's works, such as *My Antonia*, depict the regionalism of the Deep South.

   C. Emily Dickinson gained national recognition during her lifetime for the publication of over 300 poems.

   D. Upton Sinclair's writings, such as *The Jungle*, represent the optimism and trust of the American citizenry for its government.

78. Which of the following is the least preferable strategy for teaching literature?

   A. teacher-guided total class discussion

   B. small group discussion

   C. teacher lecture

   D. dramatization of literature selections

79. Which event triggered the beginning of Modern English?

   A. Conquest of England by the Normans in 1066

   B. Introduction of the printing press to the British Isles

   C. Publication of Samuel Johnson's lexicon

   D. American Revolution

80. Which of the following is not true about the English language?

   A. English is the easiest language to learn.

   B. English is the least inflected language.

   C. English has the most extensive vocabulary of any language.

   D. English originated as a Germanic tongue.

81. Which of the following is not a technique of prewriting?

   A. Clustering

   B. Listing

   C. Brainstorming

   D. Proofreading

82. **Which of the following is not an approach to keep students ever conscious of the need to write for audience appeal?**

    A. Pairing students during the writing process

    B. Reading all rough drafts before the students write the final copies

    C. Having students compose stories or articles for publication in school literary magazines or newspapers

    D. Writing letters to friends or relatives

83. **The Elizabethans wrote in**

    A. Celtic.

    B. Old English.

    C. Middle English.

    D. Modern English.

84. **Which of the following writers never won the Nobel Prize for literature?**

    A. Gabriel Garcia-Marquez of Columbia

    B. Nadine Gordimer of South Africa

    C. Pablo Neruda of Chile

    D. Alice Walker of the United States

85. **The children's literature genre came into its own in the**

    A. seventeenth century.

    B. eighteenth century.

    C. nineteenth century.

    D. twentieth century.

86. **Recognizing the quality of empathy in literature is a/an**

    A. emotional response.

    B. interpretive response.

    C. critical response.

    D. evaluative response.

87. **Which of the following should not be included in the opening paragraph of an informative essay?**

    A. Thesis sentence

    B. Details and examples supporting the main idea

    C. A broad general introduction to the topic

    D. A style and tone that grabs the reader's attention

88. **What is the figure of speech present in line one below in which the dead body of Caesar is addressed as though he were still a living being?**

   "O, pardon me, though bleeding piece of earth
   That I am meek and gentle with these butchers."
   Marc Antony from Julius *Caesar*

   A. Apostrophe

   B. Allusion

   C. Antithesis

   D. Anachronism

89. **What is the prevailing form of discourse in this passage?**

   "It would have been hard to find a passer-by more wretched in appearance.
   He was a man of middle height, stout and hardy, in the strength of maturity; he might have been forty-six or seven. A slouched leather cap hid half his face, bronzed by the sun and wind, and dripping with sweat."

   A. Description

   B. Narration

   C. Exposition

   D. Persuasion

90. **In most phases of writing, the most serious drawback of using a computer is**

   A. the copy looks so good that students tend to overlook major mistakes.

   B. the spell check and grammar programs discourage students from learning proper spelling and mechanics.

   C. the speed with which corrections can be made detracts from the exploration and contemplation of composing.

   D. the writer loses focus by concentrating on the final product rather than the details.

91. **A youngster, watching a movie in which a train derailed, exclaims, "Wow, look how many cars fell off the tracks. There's junk everywhere. The engineer must have really been asleep." Based on Piaget's beliefs about child moral judgments, the fact that the child is impressed by the wreckage and assigns blame to the engineer indicates that he is approximately**

   A. ten years old.

   B. twelve years old.

   C. fourteen years old.

   D. sixteen years old.

92. **Oral debate is most closely associated with which form of discourse?**

    A. Description

    B. Exposition

    C. Narration

    D. Persuasion

93. **Most of S. E. Hinton's novels - *The Outsiders* - are written on the sixth grade reading level. They have the greatest reader appeal to**

    A. sixth graders.

    B. ninth graders.

    C. twelfth graders.

    D. adults.

94. **Which aspect of language is innate?**

    A. Biological capability to articulate sounds understood by other humans

    B. Cognitive ability to create syntactical structures

    C. Capacity for using semantics to convey meaning in a social environment

    D. Ability to vary inflections and accents

95. **Which of the following titles is known for its scathingly condemning tone?**

    A. Boris Pasternak's *Dr. Zhivago*

    B. Albert Camus' *The Stranger*

    C. Henry David Thoreau's "On the Duty of Civil Disobedience"

    D. Benjamin Franklin's "Rules by Which A Great Empire May be Reduced to a Small One"

96. **Which of the following is not a theme of Native American writing?**

    A. Emphasis on the hardiness of the human body and soul

    B. The strength of multi-cultural assimilation

    C. Contrition for the genocide of native peoples

    D. Remorse for the loss of the Indian way of life

97. Samuel is a bright and perceptive high school junior. He has street smarts and a persistence in speaking and writing in street language, expletives included, even when discussing readings in American literature. Arthur Dimmesdale is an "uptight dude" whose "pecker" did the natural thing. If the teacher is to influence Samuel's formal communication skills, he should

   A. ask Samuel to paraphrase his writing, that is translate it, into language appropriate for the school principal to read.

   B. refuse to read Samuel's papers until he conforms to a more literate style.

   C. ask Samuel to read his work aloud to the class for peer evaluation.

   D. rewrite the flagrant passages to show the Samuel the right form of expression.

98. Which of the following contains an error in possessive inflection?

   A. Doris's shawl

   B. mother's-in-law frown

   C. children's lunches

   D. ambassador's briefcase

99. Homer's *Iliad* and *Odyssey* are taught in different grade levels from state to state and district to district. Which of the following would be the most significant factor in approaching the teaching of these classic works wherever they appear in the curriculum ?

   A. Identifying a translation on the appropriate reading level

   B. Determining the students' interest level

   C. Selecting an appropriate evaluative technique

   D. Determining the scope and delivery methods of background study

100. A punctuation mark indicating omission, interrupted thought, or an incomplete statement is a/an

   A. ellipsis.

   B. anachronism

   C. colloquy.

   D. idiom.

101. In the phrase "the Cabinet conferred with the president," Cabinet is an example of a/an

   A. metonym

   B. synecdoche

   C. metaphor

   D. allusion

102. The technique of starting a narrative at a significant point in the action and then developing the story through flashbacks is called

   A. in media res

   B. octava rima

   C. irony

   D. suspension of willing disbelief

103. The inverted triangle introduction to an essay requires that the thesis sentence occur

   A. at the beginning of the paragraph.

   B. in the middle of the paragraph.

   C. at the end of the paragraph.

   D. in the second paragraph.

104. A student composition intended for providing information should contain a minimum of how many paragraphs?

   A. three

   B. four

   C. five

   D. six

105. In a timed essay test of an hour's duration, no more than ____ minutes should be devoted to prewriting.

   A. five

   B. ten

   C. fifteen

   D. twenty

106. Which of the following sentences is properly punctuated?

   A. The more you eat; the more you want.

   B. The authors - John Steinbeck, Ernest Hemingway, and William Faulkner - are staples of modern writing in American literature textbooks.

   C. Handling a wild horse, takes a great deal of skill and patience.

   D. The man, who replaced our teacher, is a comedian.

107. The students in Mrs. Cline's seventh grade language arts class were invited to attend a performance of *Romeo and Juliet* being presented by the drama class at the high school. In preparation for the performance, they should

   A. read the play as a homework exercise.

   B. read a synopsis of the plot and a biographical sketch of the author.

   C. examine a few main selections from the play to become familiar with the language and style of the author.

   D. read a condensed version of the story and practice attentive listening skills.

108. "The *U.S.S. Constitution* is the old man of the sea" is an example of

   A. allusion.

   B. simile.

   C. allegory.

   D. metaphor.

109. Which of the following sentences contains a capitalization error?

   A. The commander of the English navy was Admiral Nelson.

   B. Napoleon was the president of the French First Republic.

   C. Queen Elizabeth II is the Monarch of the entire British Empire.

   D. William the Conqueror led the Normans to victory over the British.

110. Which of the following sentences contains a subject-verb agreement error?

   A. Both mother and her two sisters were married in a triple ceremony.

   B. Neither the hens nor the rooster is likely to be served for dinner.

   C. My boss, as well as the company's two personnel directors, have earned their ten-year pins.

   D. Amanda and the twins are late again.

111. A technique used to allow students to present written ideas without interruption of the flow of thoughts is called

   A. brainstorming.

   B. mapping.

   C. listing.

   D. freewiting.

112. A formative evaluation of student writing

   A. requires a thorough marking of mechanical errors with a pencil or pen.

   B. making comments on the appropriateness of the student's interpretation of the prompt and the degree to which the objective was met.

   C. should require that the student hand in all the materials produced during the process of writing.

   D. several careful readings of the text for content, mechanics, spelling, and usage.

113. The practice of reading a piece of student writing to assess the overall impression of the product is

   A. holistic evaluation.

   B. portfolio assessment.

   C. analytical evaluation.

   D. using a performance system.

114. Modeling is a practice that allows students to

A. create a style unique to their own language capabilities.

B. emulate the writing of professionals.

C. paraphrase passages from good literature.

D. peer evaluate the writings of other students.

115. The writing of Russian naturalists is

A. optimistic

B. pessimistic.

C. satirical.

D. whimsical.

116. Most children's literature prior to the development of popular literature was intended to be didactic. Which of the following would not be considered didactic?

A. "A Visit from St. Nicholas" by Clement Moore

B. *McGuffey's Reader*

C. any version of *Cinderella*

D. parables from the *Bible*

117. Words prevalent in Poe's "The Bells" like *tolling*, *knelling*, and *tintinnabulation* are examples of

A. onomatopoeia.

B. consonance.

C. figurative language.

D. free verse.

118. Which of the following is a characteristic of blank verse?

A. Meter in iambic pentameter

B. Clearly specified rhyme scheme

C. Lack of figurative language

D. Unspecified rhythm

119. American colonial writers were primarily

A. Romanticists.

B. Naturalists.

C. Realists.

D. Neo-classicists.

120. Charles Dickens, Robert Browning, and Robert Louis Stevenson were

A. Victorians.

B. Medievalists.

C. Elizabethans.

D. Absurdists.

121. The most significant drawback to applying learning theory research to classroom practice is that

A. today's students do not acquire reading skills with the same alacrity as when greater emphasis was placed on reading classical literature.

B. development rates are complicated by geographical and cultural differences that are difficult to overcome.

C. homogeneous grouping has contributed to faster development of some age groups.

D. social and environmental conditions have contributed to an escalated maturity level than research done twenty or more years ago would seem to indicate.

122. Overcrowded classes prevent the individual attention needed to facilitate language development. This drawback can be best overcome by

A. dividing the class into independent study groups.

B. assigning more study time at home.

C. using more drill practice in class.

D. team teaching.

123. Which of the following responses to literature are middle school students not yet prepared to assimilate?

A. Interpretive

B. Evaluative

C. Critical

D. Emotional

124. Which of the following is exhibited most in the hierarchy of needs for adolescents who are becoming more team-oriented in their approach to learning?

A. Need for competence

B. Need for love/acceptance

C. Need to know

D. Need to belong

125. What is the best course of action when a child refuses to complete a reading/literature assignment on the grounds that is morally objectionable?

   A. Speak with the parents and explain the necessity of studying this work.

   B. Encourage the child to sample some of the text before making a judgment.

   C. Place the child in another teacher's class where they are studying an acceptable work.

   D. Provide the student with alternative selections that cover the same performance standards that the rest of the class is learning.

TEACHER CERTIFICATION EXAM

ANSWER KEY

1. A	26. B	51. A	76. D	101. B
2. B	27. C	52. A	77. A	102. A
3. A	28. C	53. C	78. C	103. C
4. A	29. A	54. A	79. B	104. C
5. B	30. C	55. D	80. A	105. B
6. A	31. C	56. C	81. D	106. B
7. E	32. C	57. B	82. B	107. D
8. D	33. C	58. A	83. D	108. D
9. C	34. A	59. B	84. D	109. C
10. A	35. D	60. C	85. C	110. C
11. D	36. D	61. D	86. D	111. D
12. D	37. D	62. A	87. B	112. B
13. C	38. A	63. C	88. A	113. A
14. E	39. C	64. B	89. A	114. B
15. A	40. D	65. D	90. C	115. B
16. C	41. A	66. B	91. A	116. A
17. C	42. A	67. D	92. D	117. A
18. A	43. D	68. C	93. B	118. A
19. B	44. B	69. C	94. A	119. D
20. D	45. A	70. D	95. D	120. A
21. C	46. D	71. A	96. B	121. D
22. C	47. C	72. C	97. A	122. A
23. D	48. C	73. B	98. B	123. B
24. C	49. A	74. B	99. A	124. D
25. A	50. C	75. A	100. A	125. D

ENGLISH HIGH SCHOOL

Printed in the United States
32719LVS00005B/26